s

Guide to the Future

The Time Traveller's Guide to the Future

Prediction and Decision Made Easy

Daemon Goodhope

BLOOMSBURY

To A. R.

Acknowledgements to all the
I Ching practitioners of the past.

With special thanks to Barry Smith for
his help with the prototype.

First published in 1997

Bloomsbury Publishing Plc
38 Soho Square
London, W1V 5DF

The moral right of the author has been asserted
A copy of the CIP entry for this book is available from the British
Library

ISBN 0 7475 3386 5

10 9 8 7 6 5 4 3 2 1

Designed by Malcolm Harvey Young
Typeset by Hewer Text Composition Services, Edinburgh
Printed in Great Britain by Clays Ltd, St Ives plc

Preview *The I Ching is for winners*

We all take gambles every day, the I Ching was written to help you get the odds in your favour. *The Time Traveller's Guide* was written to make the knowledge of the I Ching available to the widest possible audience.

It only takes a few minutes, then you can relax and enjoy the benefits of the wisdom of the ancients.

Powerful

The Time Traveller's Guide is a powerful oracle that can have a profound effect on your life if you want it to.

Fun

You can use *The Time Traveller's Guide* the way you want, it makes a great parlour game, something to share with a friend or just a good read in a dull moment.

Learn The Secrets

This is the first time that the secrets of the I Ching have been made available. Others editions contain deliberate errors that the Chinese masters used to conceal the truth. MAKE A BETTER WORLD.

Keeping the truth secret may have had its merits in the past, but now the fate of our race is in the balance. We must become more spiritually aware or destroy ourselves. Every time you use your *Time Traveller's Guide* you will be contributing a little to the enlightenment of humanity.

You can contact Daemon
with your stories and questions
on the Internet (the best will be
published). Go to the TTG web
page on the Large Salad site
to receive your quarterly newsletter
with details of contacts, tuition
and much more.
www.largesalad.co.uk

Contents

Introduction

The humble shrine beside the well became a
great temple,
a fine city grew up around it.
The well was forgotten and filled with mud.
Drought came and the people moved on.
The temple fell into decay
Its treasures scattered.
Later, people returned to lovingly restore the
ruins.
Yet the well remained blocked.
Now it is time to make the sweet water flow
once more.

The Time Traveller's Guide to the Future is more than just a book,
it is the best friend you will ever have. By using the *Guide*, a
link is forged with the spirit itself and a profound inner
harmony develops that subtly alters thoughts and actions
for the better. Life becomes meaningful and one enters into
a conversation that has no end and leads ever deeper into the
mysteries of an exquisite world. The *Guide* is respectful of those
who use it sincerely and it treats them as if they were royalty.
It acts as a wise old adviser. It tells you of the probable
consequences of your actions and leaves the decisions to you.
I've spent twenty-five years studying the I Ching and trying to
live my life according to its principles and practices. It has not
been easy, but I've been very successful in my quest. I have
written this book so that others may travel on the same road
with greater ease and comfort. Other editions of the I Ching,
as I have discovered to my cost, are riddled with inaccuracies

and are very unreliable. *The Time Traveller's Guide* is clear, unambiguous and easy to use. All the advice is based on the contemplation of actual events rather than theory. Hopefully, this will mean you will go further and learn more than I have. And it is not just spiritual benefit that comes from using the *Guide*. Those who know how to follow its advice will have a very real material advantage. Greater wealth and quality of life are to be had for the asking.

Instructions

What to ask?

Asking a clear, valid question is very important if you want to get a clear, valid answer from the I Ching. There are three things a question should be:

1. Relevant

The I Ching ignores trivial or irrelevant questions. Exactly what is relevant is something you have to work out for yourself. As a rule of thumb, avoid questions about your normal routine. If you happen to live in a war zone, a trip to the shops can be lethal, but most of us don't need the *Guide*'s permission to go to Tesco's.

Questions about travel, careers, relationships, social events, studies, health, money and spiritual practice are all perfectly valid.

2. Carefully framed

Spend a little time working on the wording of your question and try to make it unambiguous. It is better to ask questions in the positive, for example, 'Should I cross the Antarctic by sledge?' This is clear and positive whereas, 'Should I not cross the Antarctic, but take a job selling insurance instead?' is vague and negative.

3. Well timed

It is not a good idea to rush to the I Ching with every whim that passes through your mind. Give the matter careful thought and do some investigation first. Quite often one finds that the answer is clear without using the *Guide* at all. If there is still uncertainty then it is time to consult the *Time Traveller's Guide*.

This all may sound quite complicated, but in my experience most people who use the I Ching regularly build up a 'feel' for what to ask and when to ask it. Ultimately you must build your own relationship with the I Ching and use it the way that suits *you* best.

There are also three types of question:

1. Action Forecasts

These relate to things that you are going to do yourself. For example, 'Should I go holiday to Jamaica?' or 'Should I take the job in the jam factory?' Action Forecasts work very well when you are clear about what you are planning and have a genuine intention to follow your plan through. Generally predictions work better with things that you have had some definite contact with. For example, if you are buying a used car it is better to make a prediction after a test drive than after a preliminary phone call.

2. Time Forecasts

These relate to periods of time, as in 'What fortune will the month of May 1998 bring me?' Time Forecasts can be made for a year, a season, a month, a week, or a day ahead. Generally they are easier to interpret for the longer periods of time – years and seasons are very accurate. Months and weeks are usually pretty good, but days can be difficult to interpret, especially if not much is happening in your life and one day is much the same as another. It is not worth trying to predict more than one year ahead as there are too many possibilities in store. The text marker TIME on each path specifically relates to Time predictions, but it is still worth reading whatever type of question you are asking.

3. Third Party Forecasts

These are predictions you make about someone or something other than yourself, for example: 'Will Labour win the election?' 'Will my son pass his exams?' or 'Will my cat come home safely?' These forecasts don't always work, but some people have more success with them than others, so don't be afraid to experiment.

How to ask it

1. You need
- The eight cards supplied with this book (or ordinary playing cards numbered ace to eight).
- A quiet moment.
- A notebook and pen.

2. Before you begin
- Check that you have all eight cards.
- Calm your mind.
- Think of a question and write it down.

3. Make a prediction
- Shuffle the cards, pick one, and make a note of its number.
- Replace the card, shuffle again, pick a card, and note its number.
- Remove cards 7 and 8 from the pack and shuffle again, then pick a card to get a third and final number.

You now have three numbers, turn the page to find your destiny.

The three numbers

The House Number

The Time Traveller's Guide is divided into eight Houses. The first number tells you in which House your prediction can be found. There is some advice at the beginning of each House which is of a general nature and reflects the overall philosophy of the I Ching.

The situation number

Each House is divided into eight Situations. The second number is the number of your Situation *within* the House. Flick through the House until you find your Situation. The text will tell you something of the background to your question. The Situation's title is often particularly important in understanding the oracle.

The path number

In each Situation there are six Paths: these are the most important part of the oracle. The Path text is always the master text. The Paths are the oldest part of the I Ching, the foundations upon which it is built.

A good path in a bad situation is better than a bad path in a good situation.

Evaluating the answer

Using the I Ching is in some ways like gambling, the idea is to use the oracle to improve one's odds of success in any venture. There are three things to consider when evaluating a prediction.

1. The happy face guide

By each path are little faces, ☺, ☹, or ☺. These tell how strong your hand is.

2. The path text

This gives you advice on how best to play your particular hand.

3. The situation text

From this you learn to see your Path as part of an overall game plan.

Reacting to the answer.

There are three possible reactions to the *Guide*'s answer.

1. Inescapably apt

Most of the time the answer will be what you knew all along anyway. We delude ourselves for all sorts of reasons, but when confronted by the truth we know it well enough. Once you know what you should do, it is only a matter of deciding how it should be done.

Consider the three factors above once more for advice on the best way to proceed.

2. I'm not sure

Sometimes the text of the answer has no obvious relevance to your question. In this case it is usually best to continue as you would have, had you not consulted the I Ching. Nine times out of ten the meaning will become clear and you can act accordingly.

3. This can't be right!

Very occasionally the answer you get from the *Guide* goes completely against your instincts. In the final analysis you must rely on your own feelings and act accordingly. The process of consulting the I Ching is not infallible and it is possible to get an inaccurate answer. However, it is wise to study the advice carefully and remember it just in case it turns out to be right.

Ready to go!

You now know the basics of consulting the I Ching and should be able to evaluate the answer you have received. It must be stressed that predicting the future is an art that takes time to appreciate, even if you have the *TTG* to get you off to a flying start.

The relationship between a practitioner and the I Ching is deep and beautiful. At first there may be some confusion, but as time goes by mutual trust and understanding develop.

One should not try for too much too quickly. If you slavishly try to obey the *Guide* in the early stages, your independence may be compromised, which will weaken you.

The correct approach is to absorb the wisdom of the ancients into your inner self so that over time you find yourself acting in harmony with the I Ching quite naturally.

If you go against the advice of the oracle and have cause to regret it, the next time you get that advice it will be much easier to accept.

No great amount of self-discipline is required, the instinct of self-preservation does the work for you.

In the same way, where you have followed the advice and had success no huge effort of will is needed to repeat the experience. Best of all is when you've done something bold that you wouldn't have normally had the courage to do. After that the *Guide* becomes a treasured friend.

When you have been using the *Time Traveller's Guide* for a few years, the Situations will become like old friends. Every time you open your copy, memories and understandings of your past and future resonate in every line of text.

THE ADVICE IN THIS BOOK IS DESIGNED TO DEVELOP YOUR FREE WILL. IF USED CORRECTLY IT WILL HELP YOU MAKE DECISIONS QUICKLY AND ACCURATELY. THE GUIDE IS NEVER SUPPOSED TO REPLACE YOUR PERSONAL ASSESSMENTS, BUT TO ADD TO THEM.

Looking a little deeper

This book is essentially a 'get you going' guide to the I Ching; naturally there is a lot more to learn. The I Ching is one of the world's oldest books and its influence in China is like the influence of the Bible in many countries in the West.

However, to make best use of this book, it is necessary to understand a little of the concept of destiny that the I Ching is based on. In the West, most people fall into one of two camps when it comes to fate. There are the Fatalists, who believe that destiny is pretty much already written and that 'if the bullet has your name on it' it will get you: and there are the Rationalists, who believe there is no plan and everything happens by chance.

In the East, ideas on fate are not so black and white. It is believed that the future has already been mapped out, but that the details are not finalized until the events actually occur. This means that individuals can alter their destiny by changing their behaviour right up until the last moment. Left to chance, most of us will end up being quite ordinary; however, with the right adjustments we can soar up to a 'better self', with greater achievements and pleasures.

The aim of using the I Ching is self-improvement, the principle being that a healthy, balanced and successful person is a benefit to the world in general.

The Predictions

1. The House of Challenge

The hidden one.
All-powerful.
Swift as a hungry tiger.
Patient beyond eternity.
Under frost-clear skies
The Dragon awaits.

Challenge (the Dragon), is a master of fate, like a celestial godfather. Challenge has two faces. One is active, dynamic and capable of anything; it is the 'hungry tiger'. The other is patient, profound and manipulative; it is the great puppet-master.

In life, Challenge often takes the form of an enemy, some-one or something sent to test you. Difficulties arise that stop you doing things the way you have been. You have to make changes to avoid the problems, and by doing so, find more success than you would have expected.

Challenge offers you two chances, the easy and the hard. The easy way is offered first, but you must be quick to take advantage of it. If you fail to take advantage of the easy way, and most people do, then pressure is placed upon you. Challenge causes you problems that push you in the direction it wants you to go; this is the hard way.

Dragon people are critical and given to bullying. They have little patience with incompetence and are very good at what they do.

Situation 1.1 Meeting the Dragon

A worthy opponent.
The battle lines are drawn.
Step forward if you dare.
Do not try to defeat a superior opponent.
Rewards for the strong.
Look for assistance.

Challenge in the House of Challenge. This means that you will be very thoroughly tested. Not the most comfortable relationship, but it has dynamic potential.

If you push ahead you are likely to encounter someone or something that will test you. If you behave correctly you will be rewarded, if not you will suffer. This is what is meant by meeting the Dragon. Whether this meeting is a good idea or not is a matter for you to decide. If you really want or need to go ahead you can. In the majority of cases the risks are acceptable and success is possible.

There is an alternative strategy; if you don't go looking for the Dragon it will come looking for you. In practice this means delaying actions and decisions for a while and seeing what happens. Often a better way of attaining your goals will become clear.

As a 'time prediction' this Situation forces change, if you work with it you can set the stage for a greatly improved life.

Path 1.1/1 ☺

Hidden designs.
The Dragon sleeps beneath the water.
Stop. Wait.
The purpose becomes clear.

There is something you should know before undertaking anything. Wait a little and events will develop in an unexpected way. Soon you will be in a better position to exploit circumstances.

TIME: *Quite lively. A good time to clear away and reorganize your life, and prepare for future undertakings. Don't finalize plans or make commitments at this stage. Rest and recreation are favourable; keep an eye out for opportunity.*

Path 1.1/2 ☺

The Dragon has a game for you.
Consider your position carefully.
Look for powerful allies.

Success is possible, but it is up to you to decide if the rewards justify the effort. Often it is best to be patient; later you will get what you want without fighting for it.

TIME: *Dynamic, you can begin new projects and sow seeds of future endeavours. Face unexpected difficulties bravely, then all will go well. It is not good to hide from fate; just take precautions. Training the mind and body will prove very worthwhile. A noble project will succeed. Look for opportunities.*

Path 1.1/3 ☺

One's weakness is exposed.
The Dragon tries to hurt you.
Be active all day.
At night rest is disturbed.
If you are cunning there is no danger.

Things are not as good as you would like. You have to work harder for less reward than anticipated. Also there is a genuine risk of injury or loss. However, with caution, this path can be successfully negotiated. Don't be too competitive: make friends, not enemies,

5

of those stronger than yourself. Something may come to you if you wait until others have fought for it and lost interest.

TIME: *Dynamic, but with troubles; much work and worry. Keep your mind fixed on your ultimate objectives, then you will not lose your way. Beware of injury. Training will lead to future success.*

Path 1.1/4 ☺

The Dragon flies this way and that.
Where will it land?

Some sort of confusion is likely here. Wait and see how things develop. Be ready to act decisively once the way is clear.

TIME: *An important phase, powerful, though possibly stressful. Most things go well. Think carefully; you are in a position to make changes to your future. Do not allow petty problems to divert your energy from important matters.*

Path 1.1/5 ☺

The Dragon looks down from the heights.
Look for powerful allies.

You should go ahead with your plans though the timing should be considered carefully. 'Looking down from the heights' means taking a broad view. Try to take the easiest route to your goal.

TIME: *Active, dangerous, with important opportunities. You are in a stronger position than you realize, you may have many problems but faced with determination they will disappear. Try not to worry about everyday matters and concentrate on your long-term interests. Your spirit is strong enough to overcome obstacles.*

Path 1.1/6 ☹

Do not act like a capricious Dragon.
You will regret it.

Moving ahead too quickly is dangerous, do not act in an impulsive way.

TIME: *Uneasy and restless, you could easily get involved in something you will regret. If you behave sensibly and stick to what you know best, you will profit from this time.*

Situation 1.2 Divided

Heaven moves upward.
The earth sinks down.
All things are divided.
Hold fast to that which nourishes you.
Look for assistance.

Development in the House of Challenge. This combination works better the other way around (Challenge in the House of Development), but here the relationship is strained. The problem is that fate pulls each in different directions, this makes it difficult to act in concert.

In this Situation you often find it difficult to decide what your priorities should be. You can find yourself pulled by opposing tendencies and your resolve weakened by indecision. There is a danger that by trying to divide your efforts you will achieve nothing and morale may become dangerously low.

To avoid the danger you must have a very clear idea of what your priorities are and concentrate on them. This may upset partners, and cause some inner conflict, but it can't be helped. Be patient in dealing with work in hand and do not allow yourself to be distracted. If you follow this advice no harm will come to you. It is also possible to attain success.

Path 1.2/1 ☺

Madder is picked.
The root and leaf are not divided.
Good fortune.

On this path division is easily avoided. Madder is a grass whose root produces a red dye. The roots and leaves are so firmly attached that they can be pulled from the soil in one piece. The lesson here is that by working on something of little value (leaves) one gains something of great value (root).

In practical language this a time when an extra effort, even though you may not feel like it, produces very good results.

TIME: *Some problems, but things clear up if you work on through. Concentrate your efforts and you will be successful.*

Path 1.2/2 ☹

Endure only what must be endured.
The weak progress.
The strong are held up.

Knowing when enough is enough is not always easy. It is best to be cautious about making changes, but if you can get rid of things that have been undermining your well-being, do so.

TIME: *You can make significant progress in small matters, but leave important matters till later.*

Path 1.2/3 ☹

Divided efforts.
The ritual offering is poorly prepared,
The workers lazy.
The end is reached slowly.

This often refers to hold-ups caused by others' ineptitude. Be patient but firm. You cannot trust on the goodwill of others.

TIME: *Expect delays and set-backs, but not everything is held up so make progress where you can.*

Path 1.2/4 ☺

Unity overcomes division.
If you work for the common good
You will find friends of like mind.

If you have a good idea and are determined, you can change bad times into good. Hard work, but worth it.

TIME: *Not good at present, but you can bring about a great improvement if you work hard and look for an opportunity.*

Path 1.2/5 ☺

> First division then unity.
> Act bravely.
> Run away! Run away!
> It is better to be tied with many bonds to a mulberry tree.

This is a path out of trouble, but not an easy one. It is hard to know in advance what will be required to succeed. The way round this is to have fail-safes in place so that whatever happens you are ahead of the game. There is some danger of losing your nerve, hence the advice to tie yourself to something. 'Many bonds' means that you should have more than one plan of action ready.

TIME: *Insure yourself against failure by spreading your risks. Good for setting things to rights, be busy and purposeful.*

Path 1.2/6 ☺

> First unity then division.
> When eating ripe fruit it is easy to forget one's duty.
> Eat without burying your face.
> Good fortune.

This is not easy to understand, for it brings success in the short term but can lead to failure in the end. The reason for this is that success on this path tends to distract you from a more important purpose. The wise enjoy the benefits of this path without allowing themselves to forget their duty.

TIME: *Coming out of the shadow; you must be patient and keep steadily working through difficulties. Soon things will take a turn for the better.*

Situation 1.3 Without Plans

**Unplanned success.
Act without expecting reward.
Continue as you are.
A bad attitude is punished.
Expect the unexpected.**

Action in the House of Challenge. These two are a natural pair and they don't need to plan their actions; even their mistakes work out well.

Your instincts and feelings are correct, however your thinking may not be. Dreams of reward weaken the mind, and priorities become uncertain. To counteract this, you must act without making plans, just doing what feeling and common sense demand. Following this advice will lead to a new and more fulfilling approach to life.

The second meaning is to do with the unexpected. When you receive this Situation there are often last-minute changes, misfortunes or other surprise events. These events make you change direction, and this may seem like misfortune but in the end will work out for the best. This is another reason for acting without expectation, you can adjust to changes of direction quickly and easily.

Do things for the sake of doing them. Really good things can only be done this way. If creative people waited for promise of payment before creating, most of the greatest achievements would never have happened. This doesn't just apply to professional matters. One may paint very well as a hobby without any hope of making money from it, the knowledge of one's excellence is sufficient reward.

In this Situation generosity will be returned in surprising and pleasant ways. Remember that in dealing with people it is not always those whom you help who help you in return.

This Situation warns those with a selfish attitude that they will suffer misfortune at this time.

Path 1.3/1 ☺☺

Unexpected good fortune.
Proceed with confidence.

The outcome may not be what you expect, however in the long run your expectations will be exceeded.

TIME: *A time of surprises. Do what you think is right rather than expedient, then any losses will be recovered. If you act selfishly you will have bad luck.*

Path 1.3/2 ☺

Ploughing without thought of harvest.
Clearing the field before planning how to use it.

Things don't turn out quite as well as you would wish, but no great disasters. Carry on with plans, but make changes where necessary.

TIME: *Adequate. There are surprises in store. Just carry on and see how matters develop.*

Path 1.3/3 ☹

The cow left tethered is stolen.
You lose, the thief gains, unfair indeed.

Innocence is punished on this path. Be aware of possible bad intentions in those you deal with. Unsuitable, but not disastrous for action. Expect some losses.

TIME: *Unexpected and unfair misfortune. Keep a tight grip on your treasures. The careful will fare well.*

Path 1.3/4 ☺

No immediate gain.
The way becomes clear.
Confident and calm.

Move ahead with confidence but keep your options open. You're moving in the right direction, so keep going. There are changes to be made, but try not to lose momentum.

TIME: *Unexpected events. Keep your wits about you and you might benefit.*

Path 1.3/5 ☺

Surprise events.
When using strong medicine
Use a little cunning.

This often refers to using some powerful method for overcoming problems. Things happen in your favour quite naturally, but there is a danger that they will go off course. Use cunning to keep things going the way you want them to. Tell people what they want to hear.

TIME: *Let matters take their own course; just keep your mind on the job in hand. Keep an eye out for opportunities. Don't worry about difficulties as they will pass of their own accord.*

Path 1.3/6 ☹

Careless action.
Injury.

Your instincts are not trustworthy at this time. Use your head to avoid injury. Not much to be gained by any action.

TIME: *Difficult, restrain yourself from impulsive actions. The careful will prosper.*

Situation 1.4 Dealing with Danger

It is tempting to let matters drift.
It is tempting to succumb to the will of
others.
It is tempting to get involved.
This is the way to unhappiness.

*Good Hunting in the House of Challenge; although attracted, these
archetypes can damage each other in the long term. Good Hunting
knows all about Challenge's bullying ways, which wear Good
Hunting down. Challenge fears Good Hunting's intelligence and
scope. Challenge's power comes from focus.*

Essentially you are dealing with forces that are greater than you are.
These forces are not that friendly, which is fairly typical in the House of
Challenge. Although you are relatively weak the odds can be evened
up by a mixture of cunning and boldness, then there will be success.
Those who are foolish and careless are likely to suffer misfortune.

Each of the six paths copes in different ways. Some advise retreat,
some advance taking precautions and find good fortune.

Path 1.4/1 ☹

**The danger can be averted.
Apply the brakes quickly.
A tethered pig does not run away.**

There are dangers that you should have as little to do with as
possible. Keep calm, don't act on impulse.

TIME: *Be wary, danger that appears small now can develop into something nasty.*

Path 1.4/2 ☺

**You have fish in your bag.
Beware of doubtful companions.**

'Fish in the bag' means gain, doubtful companions mean that the
method of acquiring it may be suspect. This path has some merit,

13

but may take you away from your true path if you follow it too far.
TIME: *Things are all right for the time being, but you cannot carry on the way you are for ever. Use any gains you make to prepare a better future for yourself.*

Path 1.4/3 ☹

Walking until there is no skin on your thighs.
Failure, but no great danger.
You cannot lose a race you don't run.

Something that has been planned doesn't work out. This path is difficult and offers little prospect of gain, so avoid it if possible. If you have to go ahead, then be firm but wary; then you should at least be safe even if not successful.
TIME: *Making your way is difficult, you are in a poor position. However you should struggle on as best you can. The less you attempt the less you will fail.*

Path 1.4/4 ☹☹

Danger is close.
No fish in your bag.
Do something quickly.

This path leads to trouble. 'No fish' means that your resources will run out. You must change your plans immediately. Keep calm, act wisely and you can save yourself a lot of trouble.
TIME: *This is a bad omen for your future, but there is still just enough time to make changes in your life. Face difficult decisions bravely. Now it is time to retreat and avoid conflict.*

Path 1.4/5 ☺

The fruit is ripe.
Things are hidden from you.
Act now with heaven's blessing.

'Ripe fruit' means an opportunity that should be exploited without delay. You can find a hidden prize. Diplomacy will extricate you from a difficult situation. Even though people plot against you, their schemes are transparent and they can't hurt you if you act now. Act correctly and you will be rewarded. Travel is favourable.

TIME: *Now is the time to make changes in life. Leave old problems behind. Move onward and upward.*

Path 1.4/6 ☺

Face to face with danger.
Use your horns to clear the way.

Using the horns means use what force is necessary. This path is a window of opportunity at a difficult time. You should act decisively. Complete your plans quickly. Do what is best for you, and don't let others involve you in their schemes. Travel is favourable.

TIME: *Trouble is coming. Be ruthless and save yourself trouble later on. You can make gains and extricate yourself from old problems. Don't be afraid to go your own way. Decisive action will bring good fortune.*

Situation 1.5 Avoiding Conflict

**You are in the right, but being obstructed.
Forcing the issue will not help.
Hold only your strongest castles.
Think carefully and take advice before
acting.**

*Adversity in the House of Challenge is not a happy combination.
However, if arguments are avoided, reasonable working relations can
be established.*

Generally, in this Situation, difficulties resolve themselves if left to do
so. If you fight your corner, someone or something will cause much
more trouble than anticipated, therefore it is better not to fight.

In spite of this adversity you can still hold on to what is
unquestionably yours and quiet insistence on your minimum rights
will secure them from harm.

Path 1.5/1 ☺

**Conflict if you continue.
It is easy to stop now.
You will lose face not property.**

The less said the better. The trouble will pass. Continue with
caution; don't start anything new.

TIME: *Difficult times; you will be wronged by others, but provided you don't get
involved there is little harm they can do you. Keep your own counsel and progress
quietly.*

Path 1.5/2 ☺

**You must retreat.
No loss of face.
The enemy is clearly superior.**

Avoid disputes and people will see that you are in the right.
Continue with caution, do not start anything new.

TIME: *Difficult times; you will be aggravated and tempted to quarrel, but this would be a mistake. Quietly persevere and all will be well.*

Path 1.5/3 ☺

Know your enemy.
Take no action now.
Do not look for or accept help.

Study and research pay off. Put up with difficult situations or people until you can see a good way of getting the better of them. Continue with caution. Don't start a new project.

TIME: *Difficult times. There will be bad feeling, but arguing will not help. Hold what is yours tightly, but don't be greedy.*

Path 1.5/4 ☻

No gain from fighting.
Accept some loss.
Better in the long run.

Avoiding disputes by changing one's attitude brings good fortune. Continue with caution and don't start anything new.

TIME: *Difficult times, but don't let it worry you. Quietly persevere and all will be well.*

Path 1.5/5 ☺

The small defeats the great.
Fight and win.
Nothing can stop you.
Act quickly.

A difficult path, but worth following in a good cause. You can engage in dangerous enterprises and succeed if you make the effort. It is very important to make sure that you are on time; allow for minor delays, they could wreck your plans (I once lost an important deal because I was a little late).

TIME: *Great things can be attained if you act ruthlessly. Make sure that you are available for opportunities and to deal with problems that arise. Failure to guard your interests could be costly.*

Path 1.5/6 ☹

After fighting all day
You lose three things.
You have less than you started with.

You will exhaust yourself to no purpose if you follow this path. Don't get involved in trouble. Times are hard and you will do well to hold on to what you have.

TIME: *Difficult times. There will be bad feeling and all sorts of quarrels. You'll need the patience of a diplomat. Think carefully if you're doing the right thing in life.*

Situation 1.6 Openness

**Openly state your interests,
People will help.
A great project can succeed.
There must be perseverance as well as
enthusiasm.**

*Intensity in the House of Challenge. Intensity is brilliant, Challenge
has power, a good combination. Intensity is very friendly and this
offsets Challenge's gruff ways.*

Now is a very good time for partnerships. Get out and talk to people,
you can make good contacts. A bold move is possible, all business is
good. In this Situation, open association is recommended, secret
brotherhoods and groups that work against the common good are
unlucky. Be trusting and friendly to other people and you will be lucky.

Path 1.6/1 ☺

**With others at the gate
All is well.**

Business is good and people get on well, it is good to extend your
circle of acquaintances. Most things succeed.
TIME: *Good. Family and business go well. Look for opportunities to make new
friends.*

Path 1.6/2 ☹

**The clan looks inward.
Less than ideal.**

'The clan looks inward' suggests weakness, you can only accomplish
so much. Business is fair. Look for ways to strengthen yourself.
TIME: *Fair. Beware of exhausting your resources. Look for opportunities to meet
new people. Spend time with friends and work steadily.*

Path 1.6/3 ☹

Hide in a thicket.
Do not climb the hill yet.
Wait for three units of time.

Delay plans for now. There seems to be some danger of argument or unpleasantness here. The time to act has not yet arrived, but it's not long away, so be prepared.

TIME: *Quite good, if you're not impatient. Make preparations and contacts; spend time with friends. Work steadily.*

Path 1.6/4 ☹

The battlements are secure.
It is better to make peace.

Nothing is gained from conflict. Move forward only if there is agreement. After some initial problems a venture will be successful.

TIME: *Quite good. Settle differences and prepare for future success.*

Path 1.6/5 ☺

Murmurs of regret followed by laughter.
Look beyond the doorstep.
There is a noble road.

Things don't turn out quite as planned, which is disappointing. However, on this path there are possible long-term gains that outweigh any temporary disadvantages. This is what is meant by 'beyond the doorstep'. A mind constantly filled with petty worries will never see the opportunities that the future contains.

TIME: *Good. Look for opportunities to meet new people. Spend time with friends and work steadily.*

Path 1.6/6 ☺

Go beyond the town.
If you meet with others there will be
Good fortune.

This is a good path for travel, especially if you have business or social matters to attend to. Just about anything will go well.

TIME: *Good. Look for opportunities to meet new people. Spend time with friends and work steadily.*

Situation 1.7 Seeking Refuge

Times of decline.
Pushing ahead brings you into danger.
It is time to seek refuge.
Who to take, who to leave behind?
Let duty be your guide.

Firm Purpose in the House of Challenge. Firm Purpose is too strong for Challenge to pick on, so Challenge leaves.

In summer it is nice to wander, but when winter draws near it's time to settle down. This Situation is about retreating, at least for the time being. Make yourself secure in advance of circumstances. There is no need to rush the preparation for winter; the seasons are quite predictable. Decide where and to whom your duty lies, then act to fulfil it. If you're asking about some plan or scheme, it's almost always better to abandon it.

The question of what to save is critical. If one plans well in advance and executes the retreat properly then little is lost. Poor planning will increase loss, which is why duty should be uppermost in one's mind.

The first three paths are involved in saving as much as possible. The last three can more or less walk away.

Path 1.7/1 ☹

Slow retreat.
Stuck at the tail of the army.
Some danger.

An uncomfortable path, not to be followed out of choice. Sometimes it means you should abandon plans and deal with something you're neglecting. Duty may seem dull, but it must be attended to.
TIME: *Low in morale and not much chance of achievement. Retiring would be good. On the plus side this is a safe enough time if you live quietly.*

Path 1.7/2 ☺

Retreating with others.
Bound together with yellow oxhide
Nothing can separate them.

You might like to advance, but you are bound to other duties ('yellow oxhide'). These must be fulfilled before you can move on.
TIME: *Not much chance of achievement. Your position is weak, but relatively secure.*

Path 1.7/3 ☺

Anxious retreat.
Take the servants,
They will bring good fortune.

When things get rough it is tempting just to abandon everything and give up. In this case you have much to lose and should continue trying to salvage what you can, even if this is very stressful. When things improve you will find your 'servants' (could be things or people) of use again.
TIME: *A lot of troubles and upsets, not too serious provided you maintain your direction.*

Path 1.7/4 ☹

Accepting the inevitable
One finds refuge.
The strong are lucky.
The weak suffer.

Advance is no longer possible and retreat is the only sensible course. You can find a place of safety if you act decisively, but if your efforts are half-hearted you will have problems. You may be worried about the consequences if you don't go along with other people's plans. However, withdrawing now will be easier than you might think. Someone who goes away does not come back.
TIME: *Quiet, without any great opportunities, but a good time to press ahead steadily. Don't foster any grand schemes.*

Path 1.7/5 ☺

Successful retreat.
All in agreement.
Calmly continue.

Here one backs out quite easily and it is clear what has to be done.
TIME: *A good time for quietly getting on with things of a practical nature.*

Path 1.7/6 ☺

Happy refuge.
One finds another way.

On this path, what starts as a retreat turns out to be an advance in another direction. Generally best to remain quiet, but a trip to the mountains might be an idea.
TIME: *A good time to take up study, go on holiday to somewhere that you might be able to live or generally advance toward a better life.*

Situation 1.8 Soft Shoes

Success through sensitivity.
The tiger sleeps.
Stay calm, move softly.
You can even tread on his tail.

Escape in the House of Challenge. Escape prefers to steal around Challenge's house when he is asleep, that's why soft shoes are a good idea.

In this Situation it is good to examine options without becoming committed. It often refers to things that are best in small measure.

'Sensitivity' means to observe someone's moods and note their reactions. When speaking, watch out for small signs of displeasure and steer the conversation in another direction. This is only possible if one has no personal axe to grind.

This is not an easy Situation, there are all kinds of dangers that you don't have the power to deal with. The tiger is very dangerous, but less intelligent than a human. In life this means remaining calm and using cunning, diplomacy and good humour to overcome difficulties. Once you have mastered these skills, you can even play jokes on those stronger than you quite safely. Now is the time to practise.

Path 1.8/1 ☺

Plain shoes.
Simple actions.
Moderate success.

On this path one can be quite straightforward. 'Plain shoes' symbolize honest intentions, which in this case are appropriate. Avoid danger by being inconspicuous.

TIME: *Not easy, but progress can be made. Be sure to keep on the right side of important people.*

Path 1.8/2 ☺

> **Walking in darkness.**
> **Soft shoes, smooth path.**
> **Patience brings good fortune.**

'Walking in darkness' implies that there are dangers you cannot see. A 'smooth path' means taking the easy way out of trouble. Not good for a new project.

TIME: *No great success. Some cunning required; keep your cards very close to your chest. Some good pickings for the careful.*

Path 1.8/3 ☹

> **Heavy shoes.**
> **One eyed, lame and clumsy.**
> **The tiger will eat you if you are not careful.**

Things can go wrong on this path, but they don't have to. If you are aware of the things that impede you they can be compensated for, then you can be successful.

TIME: *A very delicate touch is needed to avoid danger. Apologies cost nothing.*

Path 1.8/4 ☺

> **Soft shoes and careful footsteps.**
> **The tiger stays sleeping.**

With suitable caution, progress is possible.

TIME: *No great success but there are good pickings for the careful.*

Path 1.8/5 ☺

> **Quick footwork saves the day**
> **While the tiger is distracted.**
> **The goal is clear.**

Difficult problems can be managed effectively.

TIME: *You have many problems, but with careful planning and timely execution you can overcome them.*

Path 1.8/6 ☺

Fine shoes.
Bold, but discreet.
The animosity has passed.

The tiger is in a good mood and ordinary courtesy is sufficient to ensure good relations. Most matters go well.

TIME: *Good. Much can be achieved by charm and intelligence.*

2. The House of Development

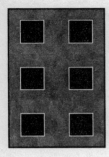

The seed that finds good earth grows quickly.
Its roots push ever deeper and it becomes secure.
When its time is finished it returns to the soil.

This is a passive House, it simply provides space for things to happen. Earth is itself neutral; if no seed is planted there will be no growth. Most of the Situations in this House represent conditions where growth can flourish and efforts are rewarded. So in spite of its receptive nature Development usually means that you should be decisive and thorough in all your dealings. There is, however, a darker side to this House, for the earth is both a womb and a tomb, the place where we come from and where we will return.

Situation 2.1 Power

Power comes after effort.
You must know when to stop.
The unworthy slowly leave
The worthy then take their place.
A moment of danger.
The way becomes clear.

Challenge in the House of Development. This is an admirable arrangement, these two balance each other perfectly. Challenge is active and strives upward, while Development is passive and downward moving; they meet in the middle.

It takes great efforts to get things the way you want them; it takes subtlety to keep them that way. In this Situation things are very nearly right, but there is one last difficult moment before you can enjoy the benefit of your labour. You must steady yourself and take stock, then do what has to be done with resolution. Whatever your troubles are, let them be and they will pass, just concentrate on what is really important to your well-being.

This Situation brings you success and pleasure in most things you might wish to do. There is a danger of a last-minute slip-up preventing something good happening (like breaking your leg foolishly before going on holiday). The danger comes from over-enthusiasm. Be aware and use only minimum force then there will be no injury. Purchases will prove good value.

Path 2.1/1 ☺☺

The roots are secure.
Growth is rapid.
You will be lucky.

A new start goes well. Anything you do will be successful.

TIME: *This is a very good time and you should make full use of it both at work and play. If you've been in trouble you can free yourself, if you have good plans they will be successful.*

Path 2.1/2 ☺☺

Treat tiresome people with tolerance.
Cross the river with confidence.
Be mindful of what seems far away.
Keep your own counsel.
Follow the middle path.
This is the way of lasting good fortune and renown.

This is a very successful path and provided you can get on it safely all will go well. Follow this advice and maintain your good fortune for as long as possible. A purchase will prove of value.

TIME: *Very good, all goes well. Put new plans into action; be bold.*

Path 2.1/3 ☺

The broad, flat path becomes a mountain track.
A fine city will one day be dust.
Remember this, but be not sad.
Treasure and prolong the gifts of life.

If there is something you are trying to do, do it soon. Take up any chance to enjoy and experience life. The good fortune here is short-lived.

TIME: *Good at the moment, enjoy it, but without forgetting that good things come to an end. Make the most of any opportunity.*

Path 2.1/4 ☺☺

Flies high without boasting.
Does not neglect friends.
Work for the common good.
Honesty and sincerity bring good fortune.

Success is assured, provided one does not become arrogant and upset people. Everyone must share the benefits, then there will be no cause for rancour.

TIME: *All is well, build friendships, and goodwill.*

Path 2.1/5 ☺☺

The King gives his daughter in marriage.
All prosper. Very good fortune.

Fate smiles upon you, anything you do can succeed. Those above you will make you one of them.

TIME: *Very good, all goes well. Start new ventures, travel or do anything exciting.*

Path 2.1/6 ☺

The city wall collapses.
The army leaderless.
There is nothing to be done.

Here this favourable Situation ends and trouble begins. Things are not that bad though and with caution a reasonable result can be obtained.

TIME: *If you are cunning in your dealings you can avoid most of the troubles that afflict those around you.*

Situation 2.2 Confinement

Act like a mare, strong, tireless, yet patient and kind.
Great plans cannot be put into effect.
Co-operation wins friends,
Competition makes enemies.
It is better to follow than lead.
It is good to work for someone.
Advancing brings misfortune, retreat is blessed. Find happiness at home.

Development in the House of Development. Here the passive nature of Development predominates and growth is stunted. Too much negativity and darkness.

One's life is restricted in some way and this must be accepted at least for some time to come. Working within the limitation can prove successful, for example, a convict who studies hard can qualify to become a respectable citizen.

Although there are restrictions, there can be benefits. Trade is often good (Development is associated with harvesting) and working within limits brings success in many fields.

There is a dark side of Development, the Grim Reaper, so beware of sickness, avoid travel and don't start anything new.

Path 2.2/1 ☹

First frost of winter underfoot,
Soon there will be solid ice.
Take measures to protect yourself now.
Prepare for a hard winter.

This often refers to an apparently minor problem that drags on and on. In fact, if it's neglected it could do you serious harm. Fortunately, the matter hasn't progressed far and preventative measures are still possible. If these are done thoroughly then the danger will be averted. Something on offer will not be all that it is cracked up to be.

33

TIME: *Danger ahead. Think very hard about what problems may occur; money and health are obvious candidates, but also a relationship may break down. Put preventative measures in place early and avoid misfortune.*

Path 2.2/2 ☺

Confinement in a great square field.
Patiently continue, be at peace.

Your freedom is not too badly restricted. By steadily practising your strengths you will gradually become expert and in time win worldly renown. However, you should attempt nothing at the moment. New projects will fail and travel is inadvisable. Existing projects prosper.
TIME: *Be quiet and restful. If you are rich you will get richer, if you are poor you won't starve. Studies go very well; be peaceful and work steadily. It's a good time to be with friends and family.*

Path 2.2/3 ☹

Hidden danger,
If you have tasks, make sure
They are completed,
Otherwise do nothing.

Be around to deal with unexpected difficulties. People may tell lies and try to create discord around you. Stay alert and you should have no problem keeping trouble at bay. Complete any project to a very high standard, or it will not be well received. A new project fails, finish one thing before starting another. Your affairs may be held up because of a misfortune that befalls another.
TIME: *This is a very good time for putting old mistakes right. You will be working at a disadvantage, but there's no help for it; quietly continue. Studies and business go quite well. Now is a good time to unravel tangled and knotty problems.*

Path 2.2/4 ☹

Tied up in a sack,
But not harmed.

If things are less than perfect, just make the best of it. A smile overcomes difficulty. You can achieve only limited success, but things could be a lot worse.

TIME: *Do not attempt anything major. Put up with limitations and continue resolutely on your path, then this time will be of benefit.*

Path 2.2/5 ☺

Confined in pleasant circumstances.
Like a minister wearing a yellow garment.
All prosper around you.

Strike a good balance between your own interests and those of others. Honest, unselfish actions win rewards. A trusted mediator can make matters prosper without really doing that much work. Balance work and rest in your own life. A 'yellow garment' was a mark of authority given to someone thought capable and fair. Starting something new yourself will fail, working for someone else will succeed. A gathering will be successful.

TIME. *You are in a secure position and will do very well in studies, business and personal matters. This is provided you stay calm and keep to your priorities.*

Path 2.2/6 ☹

If dragons quarrel in confinement
Blood is spilt.
A great pity when the end is in sight.

The period of limitation draws to an end, but for the time being you must accept things as they are. Grumbling and protesting will only lead to disaster. Beware of arguments and don't let your emotions get the better of you. A quarrel will only make matters worse; it is better to back down. If you stop what you're doing and take a break you will avoid something unpleasant.

TIME *This is a dangerous time, but provided you keep quietly getting on with your life, you should escape any great harm. If you're sensible, you can look forward to better times.*

Situation 2.3 Come Back

Going forward leads to misfortune.
Resting renews your strength.
Friends gather round gladly.
After seven units of time you can advance again.

Awakening in the House of Development. Even the restless
Awakening must relax sometimes and the House of Development is
the perfect place. The sun at winter solstice begins to strengthen, even
though it's a long time till spring (Action's season). In the same
way, you must hold back and grow strong until your season comes.

You often get this Situation when you are about to make a mistake, which is however quite easily avoided. The way out of trouble is simple, don't do anything for a while, just rest. Make yourself as comfortable as possible and just let life tick over for a while and you will find yourself strengthened, revitalized and ready to take on the world again. Happy times spent with family and friends greatly aid the recovery process. So don't travel, there will be trouble with the trip or something bad will happen while you're away.

There are two alternative interpretations which mainly apply if you are asking about time (for example; 'What will next month be like?').
1. If material things have been going badly for you they will begin to improve. Provided you don't try too much too soon a genuine renewal of your fortunes will slowly but steadily take place.
2. If material things have been good, getting this Situation means that you should concentrate more effort on your spiritual development, particularly helping others. If you fail to do this your good luck will evaporate.

Path 2.3/1 ☺

A short distance from the path.
It is easy to step back on.

You often get this at the early stage of plans; it means that you should abandon them. In all cases remain as you are.

TIME: *If you have been living by your principles you've no cause to worry. If not, you must think how to return to them. Illness and trouble clear up without intervention. Take life easy, the more you relax the more you'll benefit. Avoid travel.*

Path 2.3/2 ☺

**Quietly returning to the path.
All goes well.**

Wrong directions can be avoided quite easily. Just quietly abandon your plans and no one will mind too much.

TIME: *This is often a time of recovery, or building up strength. There is a danger that impatience will cause you to act before you are ready. Take life easy, see friends and generally consolidate your position. Illness and trouble clear up on their own. Avoid travel.*

Path 2.3/3 ☹

**Unwilling return.
There is no real option.
Danger.**

You may feel you need to continue, but this isn't a good idea. Abandoning your plans will cause some complication, but it must be so. There's a danger of being faltering and indecisive. Don't do anything or go anywhere.

TIME: *Difficult. You have strayed from your path and must return to it or suffer misfortune. This is a time to take stock of your life and think what it's all about. It isn't good to be greedy, do what you do for the love of it.*

Path 2.3/4 ☹

**One walks with others
Then returns home alone.
Small accidents.**

The support that you count on in times of trouble may fail. Make your own arrangements. Avoid engagements, new projects and travel.

TIME: *You have strayed from your path and must return to it or suffer misfortune. This is a time to take stock of your life and think what it's all about. If you let matters take their course all will be well. It isn't good to be greedy; do what you do for the love of it.*

Path 2.3/5 😐

Tardy return.
There will be no regret.

Do not do anything or go anywhere. Even though you may be quite advanced in your plans it's better to abandon them.

TIME: *You have strayed some distance from your path and must return to it. Although this might seem humiliating, in the end you'll be glad. This is a time to take stock of your life and think what it's all about. Troubles will clear up of their own accord if you take things easy.*

Path 2.3/6 ☹

Losing the path.
An army will be defeated.
Act foolishly and you will be confined for
Ten units of time.

This path is the furthest from the beginning and therefore has the most steps to retrace. This means that there is a danger of losing the path altogether. The danger is made worse if you foolishly try to use force to overcome difficulties; if you do, a period of sustained difficulty lies ahead. The right thing to do is to abandon your goals and return to the old way. Take life easy and troubles will clear up by themselves.

TIME: *You are about to make a big mistake. It seems too late to back out, but you must be ruthless and go no further. If this causes some upset, it can't be helped; it's better that others be put out than you suffer misfortune.*

Situation 2.4 The Bamboo Shoot

**A Bamboo shoot pushes rapidly upward
Taking nourishment from the earth.
Pushing hard wins rewards.
If you are confident, powerful people will
help you.
There is danger, but no need to fear.
Travelling south is favoured.**

*Good Hunting in the House of Development. Good Hunting grows
very rapidly in this House, soon it becomes so strong it can escape.*

Bamboo grows forcefully with great speed and the idea here is that
you should copy the bamboo to make good use of this favourable
Situation. Rewards can be won by hard work and taking risks; it
isn't an easy ride. It's good to push yourself beyond your usual
limits, because the use of power now will secure lasting benefit.

The Chinese put south at the top of their maps, so travelling south
represents a direct rise from obscurity. Being the warmest and most
pleasant area, the south is associated with success. If you receive this
forecast things may not be going well at present, but an ambitious
project will save you from the rut you are in. Take risks boldly: fate
loves the brave, and so do important people.

Path 2.4/1 ☺☺

**Rapid growth.
Big steps with confidence.
All obstacles overcome.
You will be lucky.**

Move boldly and don't be put off by difficulties, they will fade before
resolute action. With hard work a project will result in lasting
success.

TIME: *You may well face all kinds of problems, but there are opportunities to
make long-term improvements. Make changes, do something you've always
wanted to do while you have the chance.*

Path 2.4/2 ☺☺

> Small steps serve a great purpose.
> A humble offering is accepted
> When the sentiment is sincere.

Your true worth will be recognized and honest efforts rewarded. A great effort from a humble person is better than a half-hearted effort from someone powerful.

TIME: *Many problems, but good prospects. Take things one at a time and put in plenty of effort, then there will be success. A new project will get you out of old problems.*

Path 2.4/3 ☺

> Step quickly.
> The road is clear,
> The city without defence.

You can gain easy but not enduring success. A journey will be smooth.

TIME: *A good time to make changes and break out of a rut. There is an opportunity that should be exploited; it won't be permanent in itself, but may lead you on to something better. This is a transitional phase.*

Path 2.4/4 ☺☺

> Climbing the Holy mountain.
> Befriended by a ruler,
> Honoured at a ceremony.
> You are indeed fortunate.

A good effort will get a good reward. You may be befriended by someone powerful who helps you out of difficulty. There may be some delay involved. Don't be afraid of difficult or painful things, in the long run they will be worth it.

TIME: *Many things in your life need attention, now is the time to put them right. Someone may offer assistance that you would do well to take.*

Path 2.4/5 ☺☺

**Taking giant steps
The road is clear.
Great effort, great progress.**

You can make very good progress, and should stop at nothing. Act with determination and doggedness and you'll be very successful. You can attain a major goal; don't rest until you've gone all the way.

TIME: *Hard work on a project close to your heart will bring great success. Break away from old bad habits.*

Path 2.4/6 ☺

**Big steps into darkness,
Great progress while the light remains.**

The day is ending, an era passes, but there are still gains to be made. Bring matters to completion, but think twice before starting anything new. Unorthodox methods may be justified to exploit this brief window of opportunity.

TIME: *Bring a phase of life to successful completion, you have the chance to make gains. Secure the present, then you can plan for the future.*

Situation 2.5 Attack

Like a soldier
Be strong and in the middle.
Decisive action wins the day.
The battle is won.
The war continues.

*Adversity (water) builds up in the House of Development, then
suddenly it bursts the banks and escapes.*

A rapid response often gets you out of danger and wins rewards in
this Situation. Being 'strong and in the middle' means not losing
your head. Attaining the right mix of fluent action with cool
calculation is the key to success.

The long-term benefits of this Situation are less certain, act now
for immediate gain and consider the future later.

Path 2.5/1 ☹

Ill-considered advance.
You need to prepare.
If you go ahead now you will lose.

Rethink your strategy, either this is a poor idea or it needs much
better planning. Continue with care.

TIME: *A frustrating time: you may have all sorts of plans, but don't go ahead
with anything new just yet. Now it's good to plan and prepare. Be energetic
dealing with old problems and get your life up to date.*

Path 2.5/2 ☺

In the middle of an army
One escapes harm, and is honoured.

Action now will bring rewards, the middle of the army is generally
where the officers like to be. Officers are also well known for winning
honour without doing too much fighting. The cunning Adversity
knows how to look after number one.

TIME *Be energetic and you will be rewarded.*

Path 2.5/3 ☹☹

Corpses in the wagon.
The army commanded by fools.

Either the officers are dead and the fools have taken over, or the officers were fools in the first place. This is a pretty bad path, get off it.

TIME *A bad omen, something unexpected and very unwelcome will happen soon. Think carefully; it isn't too late to avoid the danger if you can only work out what it will be. Often it's something you have relied on too heavily that lets you down.*

Path 2.5/4 ☺

A retreat in good order.

Back off. There is nothing to be gained at present. The only kind of action that might be appropriate is some form of relaxation or holiday.

TIME: *Take a back seat, retire or take a holiday. Restrain yourself and don't become involved in any kind of conflict. This is a good time to be busy on something other than your usual pursuits.*

Path 2.5/5 ☺

When there is game it can be caught.
When there is danger you can escape it.
Do not expose the weak to danger.

This path offers great success. Be bold even if you are at a disadvantage. If you're in trouble, now is the time to get out of it. However this path is tiring, be sure that the prize is worth the effort. Lastly, be very careful if you have helpers; don't expose those who are weak or inexperienced to risk.

TIME: *Great success is attainable. Now is the time to make great efforts and take big risks to do something really worthwhile.*

Path 2.5/6 ☺☺

The war is over.
The ruler divides the spoils.
The good are rewarded with office.
The bad given money.

This path is safe and fortunate; anything you have in mind is worth pursuing. Even doubtful people must be rewarded for their efforts, but it's better that they have only cash, if they had office they might abuse it.

TIME: *Great success, nothing to worry about, everything goes smoothly. A good time to do something you've always wanted to do.*

Situation 2.6 Hide Your Light

The Light darkens.
A destructive power stalks the land.
You will be injured unless you hide.
Do not despair.
Limit the damage.
Wait until the darkness has passed.

Intensity in the House of Development, a bad combination. Intensity (light) can be damaged by Development (darkness). However darkness can also be a hiding place.

This situation always means injury of one sort or another. Otherwise good plans fail and people you usually get on with turn against you; even your health may let you down. In some way or other injury will try to find you. Darkness means that it's hard to see the danger until it's too late. You must keep calm, everyone has unlucky times, it's nothing personal and because you know in advance there's much that can be done to limit damage. How great the injury is usually depends on how important what you are doing is. A large project failing has much worse consequences than a small one. The injuries caused by motor racing are worse than those of tennis.

The first thing is to cut your exposure to risk; postpone or cancel arrangements. Avoid quarrels, you will lose out. Get involved in some quiet pursuit. When this bad time has passed everything can get back to normal, provided you have avoided any great injury.

Path 2.6/1 ☹

No good place to hide.
Do not rest for three units of time.
Do not be influenced.
In the end you will have good luck.

If you have to follow this path you will suffer for a while and must make great efforts. Stick to what you know is right for you, even though people may try to pressure you into abandoning your quest. In the end you will find what you are looking for.

TIME: *Dangerous, take precautions. You are in an uncomfortable situation with many difficulties, it may well be that you should look for a way to escape.*

Path 2.6/2 ☹

Wounded in the thigh
A horse will die for its rider.

Not a good path to follow if you can help it. Sometimes this means that something you do will be of great help to someone else but will do you harm. Think carefully.

TIME: *Dangerous, take precautions. Be conscious of what you do for other people, and how much you are prepared to suffer for them. You must be very careful to keep out of trouble. Get on with your essential tasks only, when things get better no great damage will have been done.*

Path 2.6/3 ☹☹

Escape to the south.
Look for help.
Do not expect improvement too soon.

Avoid this path, it leads to injury; you should look for alternatives. The south often represents home, comfort and easy living. If help is available, take it.

TIME: *You will be harmed if you continue as you are; try to take evasive action. At least keep out of harm's ways as much as possible, it is better to be frustrated than injured. Remember, this time will pass.*

Path 2.6/4 ☹

Injured in the stomach.
Follow your heart.
Escape from the courtyard.

Avoid this path if possible and look for alternatives. Trust your instincts.

TIME: *Danger threatens and you must get out of harm's way. Use your instincts to decide how to act. This time will pass and things go back to normal, as long as you can avoid injury now.*

Path 2.6/5 ☹

Like a ruler in danger
Others will fall with you.
Act to protect everyone's interest.

Avoid this path if possible and look for alternatives. This Path is commonly about being in a responsible position at times of crisis. If it were only your interests at stake you could get out of danger easily, but sometimes you must consider others. Traditionally this is associated with Wen of Chou, who was imprisoned by the tyrannical Shang. He submitted to and even humoured his captors while planning their eventual overthrow.

TIME: *Nothing will be successful. Delay or abandon plans. Remember this bad time will pass and you can continue, provided you avoid injury now.*

Path 2.6/6 ☺

First darkness then light.
The unworthy ones who climbed toward heaven
Now fall to earth.

The darkness is passing, but the unlucky time has not finished yet. Delay actions.

TIME: *The time of injury is nearly ended. You can begin to make plans and be active again. Do not let your guard down until you are certain the danger has passed. Make sure you do a thorough job in uprooting weeds from the garden of your life. Long-standing problems can be resolved over this period, make sure this happens.*

Situation 2.7 Worthiness

**Be modest, but know your worth.
Your confidence is less than your ability.
Take what is on offer graciously.
There is no shame in asking for that which
you deserve.**

*Firm Purpose in the House of Development. These two understand
and complement each other perfectly.*

Here we have instruction on how to balance modesty with pride.
Someone who has no pride in themselves will always be miserable,
someone who has no modesty in dealing with others will always be
disliked. You must learn to stick up for your rights without
becoming arrogant. In many societies there is a tendency to punish
anyone who tries to follow their own path. This makes people far too
timid when it comes to standing up for what they believe in. At this
time, however, a straightforward, honest approach will get a fair
hearing.

So don't be shy, when something you want is available to you take
it immediately. If people give you something they expect a little
reticence, but get angry if their gift is not accepted with enthusiasm.
This applies to fate as well; if you don't make the most of
opportunities now, fewer will come your way in the future.

Path 2.7/1 ☺

**Doubly worthy
You may cross a great river.**

Here, worthiness is likely to be rewarded, so put your best foot
forward. Anything you do will bring some success.
TIME: *A good time to make changes and begin new projects. Press for your own
maximum advantage.*

Path 2.7/2 ☺

Seen to be worthy
Calmly continue.

People will see when you are in earnest and respect you for it. Most matters prosper.

TIME: *You can receive rewards for straightforward honesty and hard work.*

Path 2.7/3 ☺

Worth is recognized.
It is time to move forward.
Fate has a prize for you.

Act quickly! There is much to gain. Your fate is very strong at the moment, use it well. Anything you do succeeds.

TIME: *Even if you have had bad times, you can make a new start. Most things go well. You can set up something of lasting value. Time to do what you believe is right.*

Path 2.7/4 ☺

Worthy and responsible
Move steadily forward.

Most matters prosper, be confident but thorough in your dealings.

TIME: *Good, follow your heart and use your head.*

Path 2.7/5 ☺

Worthy and powerful.
Deal firmly with friends and neighbours.
Vigorous movement brings success.

Punish troublesome people and reward good friends. Remove obstacles by force. With care most matters prosper.

TIME: *You can improve your position in life by acting strongly now. It may not be easy, but stick to what you believe in.*

Path 2.7/6 ☺

Worthiness becomes action.
Set your armies marching.
Take charge of matters that affect you.

Most things succeed if you act determinedly.

TIME: *Particularly good for bringing matters to fruition. Generally prospects are improving.*

Situation 2.8 A New Start

Winter has ended.
It is time to act.
Take control.
Make no long-term plans.
In the eighth month there will be trouble.

Escape in the House of Development. A good relationship. Escape becomes strong in this House and rapid growth is possible. In the spring, plants must escape the earth to find the light.

This is an active Situation, the start of a period of improvement. Now the prospects are very good indeed, make full use of the time. Anything new that you do will be successful. In the long term, don't forget that summer soon fades (autumn begins in September, the eighth Chinese month) and the good fortune will decline. This isn't a warning not to act now, but a reminder that you must keep finding new sources of good fortune. In any case there is a feeling of youthful joy here that is incompatible with long-term plans. Do what the moment requires and move on.

In practical terms it often means that the good fortune you receive now will be a stepping stone to something even better.

Path 2.8/1 ☺☺

A good escape.
Act quickly.

Much to be gained. This path is good for almost anything. Act now while you have the chance.

TIME: *Prosperous and pleasant with good opportunities. There may be problems later so make the most of your good fortune now.*

Path 2.8/2 ☺☺

Escape with others.
Act quickly.

Much to be gained. This path is good for almost anything. Act now while you have the chance.

TIME: *Prosperous and pleasant with good opportunities. Later there may be problems, so make the most of your good fortune now.*

Path 2.8/3 ☹

Escape is difficult,
Be cautious.

Not an easy path to assess, certainly it seems only moderate success is possible.

TIME: *Restlessness may lead to headstrong action. Be patient and matters will progress.*

Path 2.8/4 ☺

Controlling oneself.
Blameless.

There is a limit to how much can be achieved here. Through self-restraint one gains respect. Think things through and you will get a fair result.

TIME: *Fair, try to get new projects off the ground.*

Path 2.8/5 ☺

Partial escape.
Wisdom in action.
Thus a ruler controls the people.

There may be good reasons why you can't completely free yourself from trouble. 'Wisdom' tends to imply restraint and compromise. 'A ruler' is someone with responsibility to others.

TIME: *Quite positive, but affairs must be handled carefully if good fortune is to continue.*

Path 2.8/6 ☺

Completing the escape.
When you have finished, a new way will open.

Probably not a good omen for a new start, this is a path about endings, not beginnings.

TIME: *One phase is coming to an end. You should work to tie up loose ends.*

3. The House of Awakening

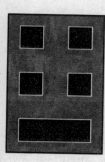

Spring thunder.
A shoot bursts free from the earth.
A plethora of beings struggle in the mud.
Fear not, the danger passes as quickly as it came.

Spring is here and it is time to get things moving. An energetic outburst puts danger behind and establishes a foothold on new territory. This is essentially a lucky house, all kinds of things can go wrong but then sort themselves out. In the end you should be better off than when you started, provided you don't lose your nerve. Being decisive is generally more important than being right in this house.

Situation 3.1 A Gap in the Hedge

A stubborn ram butts against the hedge, becoming entangled.
A wily goat jumps the hedge at its lowest point.
Use power carefully.

Challenge in the House of Awakening. A relationship between two powerful but independent personalities can be very successful, if they respect each other. Give partners room and trust them to behave sensibly and all will be well. People of genuine ability are justifiably proud and must be treated with a little deference. When two people treat each other well it brings great good fortune.

Traditionally this Situation is associated with April, the month when winter's grip is finally broken. It is an important but dangerous time; a late frost can still damage crops. The farmer must be shrewd to exploit the season to the full.

The right mixture of cunning and audacity is symbolized by the goat. Reckless, forceful behaviour, by the ram. A person who is cunning knows how to watch and wait, but this will not by itself lead to freedom. When the time comes you must act decisively or lose.

In practical terms you may well be quite successful in most matters provided arguments are avoided.

Path 3.1/1 ☺

Your toes are strong.
Is the rest of you?
Know your weakness
Then find your true strength.

The toes are weak and cannot go anywhere on their own. Make sure that you can follow through with anything you undertake. If you behave well success will come.

TIME. *Things will get better and your efforts will be rewarded if you act decisively and thoroughly.*

Path 3.1/2 ☺

A good leap.
Careful landing.

Take on what you know you can deal with and a reasonable level of success is possible. Teaming up with someone powerful could be a good idea.

TIME: *Generally positive. Move forward with quiet determination.*

Path 3.1/3 ☺

Power in the wrong hands.
The goat leaps the hedge,
But its horns become entangled.

Getting the horns stuck is bad news. A venture may fail, and the more you struggle the weaker you will be. Best to avoid this Path if possible, otherwise be extra careful to avoid potentially difficult situations.

TIME: *Difficult, and you could get into quite a lot of trouble if you are foolish and impatient. However, if you keep your nerve and quietly get on there should be no real danger.*

Path 3.1/4 ☺

The hedge begins to open.
Leave regret behind.
The big cart has a strong axle.
The destination may change, but the rule of the road is always the same.

A big cart with a strong axle can carry many things, much is possible. Here it is more important to take the right attitude than go in any particular direction. As you move ahead the way will become clear.

TIME: *Exciting. This is a time when lots of things are starting and there will be all kinds of problems, but if you press ahead steadily all will be well.*

Path 3.1/5 ☺

Unforeseen troubles come.
A shrewd, agile goat escapes.

Let matters develop before deciding how to act. Unexpected problems throw life into confusion, but there is a way out. Stay calm. Just do what you have to until the escape route is clear to you. Once you know what to do, act promptly.

TIME: *Changes are needed to avoid danger. Keep your options open and observe the situation carefully. A way to escape your problems is available if you have the presence of mind to take it; if you pull it off you will have great good fortune.*

Path 3.1/6 ☻

The goat jumps badly.
Undignified.

Trying to go that bit further causes problems, be happy with moderate success.

TIME: *Transitional and unstable. Be patient, see things through.*

Situation 3.2 Following Through

Overcome inertia.
Let not one single day pass.
Take necessary steps.
Appoint helpers.
See things through.

Development in the House of Awakening. This can work out well.
Development is very thorough, patient and hard working: Awakening
is full of energy and ambition.

This is a favourable Situation, anything that you attempt will do
well provided you tackle it with gusto. The danger is that you will
procrastinate and dither until the opportunity has passed. If you
can't act immediately then don't let a single day pass without doing
something to realize your objective.

Breaking away and doing something new will be successful.
Resolute conduct will get you out of trouble.

Path 3.2/1 ☺

Enduring intent.
Do not be content to let things slip.

This Path can be long and slow and will test your powers of
endurance and determination. The rewards are also long-term so
it can be worthwhile. It's good for studies and long serious projects.
Though the work will be hard the reward will be great.

TIME: *If you act determinedly and stick with your goals, much can be achieved.*

Path 3.2/2 ☺☺

Solid as a rock.
Act before the day is out.

Provided you fix your intent and set to work, all will go well. A very
good outlook for most things you might wish to do. If you have
troubles, hold your ground and they will pass.

TIME: *Good for achievements. Take courage. Don't let anything put you off*
doing what you know is right.

Path 3.2/3 ☺

Be enthusiastic, not lazy.
Do not wait for help.

There are some difficulties, but this must not cause you to become irresolute. Make up your own mind what to do and do it unhesitatingly. If you fail to act decisively, you will suffer misfortune.

TIME: *Unsettled. Many problems. Keep steady and don't let anything put you off doing what you know is right.*

Path 3.2/4 ☺☺

At the centre
Act with certainty
Then friends will gather round.
You can achieve much
Like hairs gathered in a clasp.

Very lucky, all will prosper. If you have troubles hold your ground, people will respect you.

TIME: *Good for achievements. Take courage. Don't let anything put you off doing what you know is right.*

Path 3.2/5 ☺

Always sick, but surviving.
Nothing to be enthusiastic about.

Not a good Path to follow. There are some quite serious problems. If you're careful you can scrape by. A new project will fail.

TIME: *Things are not good, but as long as you're careful there will be no collapse.*

Path 3.2/6 ☺

Superficial enthusiasm
Makes an attempt.
Consummation requires greater commitment.

Here Awakening's weakness shows it's good at starting, poor at finishing. This is a sixth Path, which means it's time to bring matters to conclusion.

TIME: *You will be frustrated, and not able to do what you want to, but there are affairs that need attending to before you move on.*

Situation 3.3 Hold Steady

First comes fear, Oh no, Oh no!
Then laughter, Ha, Ha, Ha.
The danger will pass.
You may let the world know.
Fate is in your favour.
Nothing will be lost.

Awakening in the House of Awakening. This can mean surprises
and not always pleasant ones. However, the danger will pass like a
spring thunderstorm and all will be well.

This is a difficult Situation to assess, because there tends to be a
surprise element and surprises are by definition difficult to predict.
What can be said with confidence is that if you suffer loss or have a
problem it will pass. This is provided you keep a cool head and don't
do anything silly. Often you end up somehow better off after the
crisis than you were before. This is in essence a lucky Situation.

Path 3.3/1 ☺

What will be will be.
Stay calm.
There is no danger.

If you have something definite in mind it will work well, but vague
plans tend to come to nothing. Fate may have its own ideas of what is
best for you, so be aware of potential opportunities. If you are in trouble
you will soon be free from it. People will help you of their own accord.
TIME: *Even if things go wrong, it will turn out in your favour in the long run.*
Very lucky for those who can keep steady.

Path 3.3/2 ☺

Action brings danger
A hundred thousand times.
Treasure is lost, do not try to hold it.
Climb nine hills.
After seven the treasure is returned.

I've no idea what the 'hundred thousand times' is about, but it sounds interesting. The rest is straightforward enough, something goes wrong and there's a lot of rushing about, then it turns out to be a storm in a teacup. In practice, plans suffer some sort of setback and maybe a change of tack is needed.

TIME: *Lucky overall. Don't allow troubles to throw you off course.*

Path 3.3/3 ☺

**Stumbling steps.
Steady yourself, or face misfortune.**

Keep a clear head and evaluate what is happening carefully. You must do this without losing momentum; tricky, but you can do it. In business, hold out for a better deal, but not for too long, or you'll lose it.

TIME: *Shocks and disturbance. Some good possibilities. Don't panic, all danger will pass. Watch out for opportunities.*

Path 3.3/4 ☹

**Even the mighty cannot run in a mire.
Delay acting.**

Delay spoils plans and there is little you can do to make things happen. Best wait and see what happens before going any further.

TIME: *Hindrances and delays leave you stuck in an uncomfortable position, but your luck will soon change and all your problems will be overcome.*

Path 3.3/5 ☺

**Running feet twist and turn.
You receive the help you need.
Very good fortune.
No danger.**

There may be twists in the tail, but overall things go better and with less effort than expected. An offer is very good. An old trouble disappears pretty much on its own.

TIME: *Even if things are bad, your luck will soon change for the better. Work goes well. This is a good time to make contacts and meet people, you are very likely to get a good offer from an unexpected source.*

Path 3.3/6 ☺

Stamping feet at the house of a neighbour.
What has not touched your body cannot harm you.
Avoid conflict.
There will be tales to tell.

Action goes on around you and you should keep calm. In practice this is quite a good Path, generally things go better than expected.
TIME: *Lucky, with some shocks and surprises.*

Situation 3.4 Duty

Wind and thunder dutifully support each other.
When travelling, go further.
When working, work harder.
Steady, constant effort.

Good Hunting in the House of Awakening. This is a practical relationship, not that exciting, like an old married couple who run a business together.

Duty is a funny thing, the definition used here is something that is not done for its own sake. For example one goes for dental work for the sake of one's teeth not for the joy of seeing the dentist. Duty is not necessarily unpleasant, riding to work through the park is duty, but on a sunny morning it doesn't feel like it. The first duty we all have is to feed ourselves properly, again this can be a pleasant or a not so pleasant experience. So you see it is pretty important to establish where your duty lies and how to fulfil it pleasurably.

In this Situation one should continue on one's path with increased effort. When travelling, push further while the going is good.

Although duty is clearly essential, and even enjoyable, it does have a wearing effect if sustained for too long. In general the best thing is to do your duty as quickly as thoroughness permits and move on.

Path 3.4/1 ☺

No clear duty as yet.
A chariot is too hasty,
Better to ride a mule.
Continue calmly.

Here things are at an early stage and it's not good to expect too much. Immediate duties should be continued while careful thought is given to future prospects.

TIME: *You may find yourself restless and at a loose end, but this must be overcome. Do what you can for now and you will get a chance to do what you want later.*

Path 3.4/2 ☺

Duty overcomes fear.
Moderate success.
Eat the game that heaven provides.
Regret vanishes.

This Path is quite successful, but lacks real enthusiasm. If it is something you need to do, this is fine.

TIME: *A good time for getting your life up to date. Not a great time but significant progress can be made.*

Path 3.4/3 ☹

The meat is better without sauce.
Keep struggling, or you will suffer.

Keep things simple. Redouble your efforts on existing projects. Do not start anything new, you have much work to complete.

TIME: *A restless time, you feel the your life at present leaves much to be desired. This makes you very prone to temptations, but keep steady and all will be well.*

Path 3.4/4 ☹☹

The larder is empty.
There is no game in the field.

Your duty here is to protect yourself. 'No game' means your resources will fail if stretched. Do not go ahead with anything or you will suffer misfortune.

TIME: *Dangerous, your luck has almost run out. Protect your family, property and health. Maybe retire or take a break from work. In dangerous times you must consider carefully the options to avoid trouble.*

Path 3.4/5 ☺☺

Duty beyond duty.
Act like a warrior not a slave.
The strong succeed, the weak stay at home.

This is good for honourable enterprises. Think again about your plans and try to make them more daring. Don't fear the opinions of others when your cause is noble. For those who are bold and disciplined there are rewards. This is a bad Path for someone who is weak.

TIME: *There is much to be done, pushing beyond your usual limits brings good fortune.*

Path 3.4/6 ☺

Restless and indecisive.
The game will be lost.

Restore discipline. You have been dithering and procrastinating too long. Deal with matters in hand promptly. Don't take on anything new.

TIME: *Restless and difficult. Be patient, you must complete old projects, later new avenues will open.*

Situation 3.5 Release

**If you are confined, now is the time to break free.
Combining resolve with caution creates
good fortune.
Danger recedes.
Do only what needs to be done.
Then rest easy.**

*Adversity in the House of Awakening The cunning of Adversity and
the boldness of Awakening working together can get you out of all
sorts of scrapes.*

This Situation often means that you can extricate yourself from
undesirable circumstances. Generally, you need to make a short
burst of energy to set up an easier, pleasanter lifestyle. Avoid things
that are likely to mean long-term stress.

Of course knotty old problems don't necessarily give up without a fight.
This is why you need both resolve and caution to extricate yourself. It's
not enough that something just gets done, it must be done properly.

Path 3.5/1 ☺☺

The path to freedom is clear.

Most things you might have in mind will succeed. Free yourself while
you have the chance. If you ask about trouble, no action is required.
TIME: *Be active. Illness and other impairments disappear. If you wish to make
changes now is a good time.*

Path 3.5/2 ☺☺

**The hunter catches three foxes.
A reward of a golden arrow.**

It is worth making the effort to do something close to your heart.
Trouble can be made to disappear, and its cause removed. If you are
planning something, it will succeed.
TIME: *Free yourself while you can. Illness and other impairments disappear. If
you wish to make changes now is a good time.*

Path 3.5/3. ☺

> **Carrying a burden weakens you.**
> **Robbers can steal your possessions.**
> **Even in a carriage you are not safe.**
> **It is best to wait.**

Things won't turn out very well, though you can avoid serious harm with care. However, taking safety measures doesn't turn failure into success. Save your strength, it's not as great as you think.

TIME: *A restless transition. It will be very tempting to make changes prematurely, or indulge in all manner of distraction. The best things is to take things slow and steady.*

Path 3.5/4 ☹

> **The big toe is hurt.**
> **Progress to freedom is delayed.**
> **It is best to wait.**

To press ahead on the road to freedom with a bad toe is clearly undesirable. Think hard about making improvements in your handling of affairs.

TIME: *Troubles will clear up towards the end, provided you haven't made more for yourself. Try to make quiet, steady progress.*

Path 3.5/5 ☺

> **The path to freedom has pitfalls.**
> **Then success will be yours.**
> **Be careful how you tread.**

There is a good chance of success here, but there are dangers. Do things properly, don't hurry or indulge in false economy. Think carefully before you act and leave good safety margins.

TIME: *Active. All kinds of old troubles can be overcome. New projects are favoured.*

Path 3.5/6 ☺

Like a great hunter
A hawk is killed.
A wall is scaled.

You can be very bold on this Path, but caution should not be thrown to the wind.

TIME: *You can clear old hindrances and move on to better things. Be active.*

Situation 3.6 Flowering

**Flowering is memorable, but brief.
Enjoy life's pleasures while you may.
The sun at midday has no thought of
evening.**

*Intensity in the House of Awakening. Neither of these archetypes are
enduring, they cause changes then move on. Awakening is associated
with vigorous growth, Intensity with hot sun, this combination
brings great abundance. Also Intensity (sun) combined with
Awakening (fast-growing plants) creates a lot of foliage which
obscures the light on some Paths, making them less favourable.*

Some things are not designed to last. The long, hot days of summer
soon pass, but only a fool worries about winter while the weather is
fine. The benefits of this Situation are only temporary, but providing you remember that castles in the sand melt into the sea, there is
no harm building them.

Flowering is the peak of the reproductive cycle, therefore one
need not be sad at its passing, for it will return. Flowers are very
delicate and easily damaged so be careful in what you do.

Path 3.6/1 ☺

**Sustainable flowering.
Meeting a kind ruler.
Ten times they work together.
Seek recognition.
No mistakes.**

The best kind of flowering. An opportunity will lead to success. Act
now while the going is good. Someone in authority will be helpful.
'No mistakes' means that even if things appear to go wrong all will
be well in the end.

TIME: *A good time to make big changes: this may mean big problems, but at this
time you can make it. A change you make now will carry on affecting you for a long
time. A prosperous time, so take on new projects and make provision for the future.*

Path 3.6/2 ☺

So abundant are the vines that there is darkness at noon.
You may meet distrust and resentment.
Use the force of truth and all will be well.

You must wait for a while, there are problems like clouds that cover the sun. When they have passed you may act.

TIME: *Things are good, but there is some foreboding, a shadow on your well-being. Be careful how you use your resources. Danger will pass before long.*

Path 3.6/3 ☺

So abundant are the vines that even at noon there is darkness.
It is better that your right arm be broken than have it used to cause harm.
Good fortune comes in its own time.

This is a Path of some confusion. An opportunity may present itself, it seems good. If it's a small matter you might well take it. However something much better will come if you wait, so it's better to avoid any long-term commitments.

TIME: *A time of mixed blessings. Use what is available, but delay long-term plans. There may be opportunities for short-term gain. A little recreation will be of benefit.*

Path 3.6/4 ☹

Brief flowering.
Darkness makes the lamp seem bright.
If a way can be found all will be well.

A complicated Path. Things go well at first, but then take a turn for the worse (what you thought was dawn turns out to be a lamp). If you can discover the nature of the problem and tackle it there may be something gained.

TIME: *Dangerous, you cannot trust that things are as they seem. Lower your profile and sit it out.*

Path 3.6/5 ☺

Hidden brightness.
Be without designs.

There is often some confusion on this Path and the meaning doesn't always come clear. However, there is no danger to speak of so you can go ahead and see what happens. Act in a modest and guileless way.

TIME: Generally good, and there may be some opportunities for the future.

Path 3.6/6 ☹

The house is overgrown.
The family cannot be seen.
Looking through the gate you see no one.
Delayed for three units.
Minor misfortune.

Things don't work out as you planned, existing arrangements cannot be used. A rather unsatisfactory alternative may be found. No great danger if you keep your head.

TIME: *A rather confused time. The 'overgrown house' suggests neglect of things close to you; if this continues you will lose sight of your 'family' altogether.*

Situation 3.7 Confusion

Mediocrity and envy.
A bird that flies too high is shot.
A bird that stays in the nest is safe.
Big plans become bogged down.
Let this time pass.

*Firm Purpose in the House of Awakening. This relationship doesn't
work. Misunderstanding leads to suspicion and envy. The slow,
steady Firm Purpose annoys the mercurial, impatient Awakening.
The result is tiresome bickering. Firm Purpose (quiet, purposeful)
gives the better example of how to behave in this Situation.*

This Situation represents a time of confusion, with mean-minded
incompetent people in charge. It is best not to attempt much at the
moment, soon this time will pass. The important thing is not to
waste your energy and resources on hopeless projects.

Here you are hampered by tiresome petty obstacles. Apparently
inconsequential things turn out to be a big nuisance. You may think
that small problems can be overcome; individually they can, but too
many too fast can cause serious trouble. The trick is not to move
ahead too fast: solve one thing at a time and the situation can be
quite productive. Hasty, thoughtless action may expose you to risk.

Honesty will not be helpful in this Situation, because mean-
minded people are in charge.

Path 3.7/1 ☺

The bird that flies injured.
Remain in the nest.

Not a Path to choose. Anything important will fail. If you must, take
it step by step. Danger can be averted with care.
TIME: *Rather frustrating. You may feel like making big changes, but if you do,
they lead to endless unforeseen problems. What is needed is a methodical,
conscientious approach. Get free from small problems and at the end of this time
you will be better placed than at the beginning.*

Path 3.7/2 ☺

A girl meets her grandmother.
A boy meets his grandfather.
It was supposed to be the other way round.
One cannot speak to the ruler.
Only a servant is available.
This cannot be helped.

A picture of confusion, but some sort of order seems to prevail in the end. The trick to avoiding it is being patient and waiting to see how things turn out before committing yourself.

TIME: *Not that much fun. If you stay quietly minding your own business, you'll come to no harm.*

Path 3.7/3 ☹

Beware.
Someone may strike you from behind.

Being 'struck from behind' might mean betrayal, ambush or any unexpected danger. These are the hardest to avoid. It is not likely to be very serious, but it's still something you could do without.

TIME: *Dangerous and unsettled. Changes need to be made and you may feel pressured into acting hastily, but this would be a big mistake. Keep your nerve, hold on to what you have and plan your moves carefully. Be careful of what you say, a 'friend' may not be what they seem. Beware of back-stabbers.*

Path 3.7/4 ☹

A meeting, but not as planned.
Leaving the nest brings danger.

Not a Path to follow if you can help it, but it can be negotiated with care if necessary. Sometimes it refers to something you are doing as a favour that turns out to be more trouble than you thought.

TIME: *A dangerous time, you must play your cards skilfully. It's not possible to escape at once, wait for the right moment and be ready. Keep your own counsel.*

Path 3.7/5 ☹

Dense clouds,
No rain.
The game has run to ground
But the hunter can still catch it.

Again a confused image, 'dense clouds, no rain' means that promises do not come to fulfilment. Getting at game that has gone to ground is possible, but is a lot of work for limited reward.

TIME: *Not much fun. If you stay quietly minding your own business you will come to no harm.*

Path 3.7/6 ☹

The connection is missed.
The bird flies off alone.
Misfortune.
This means bad luck and injury.

It will be very hard to make anything work out. Better take things easy; if you try too hard now, you'll find yourself in difficulties.

TIME: *Not very good, there is little that can be done. You must save your strength and wait for better times.*

Situation 3.8 Unequal Partnership

Unequal alliance is of benefit for a while.
Look for advancement.
Take what you can get.
Move on when the time comes
Otherwise there will be misfortune.

Escape in the House of Awakening. Awakening plays the petty tyrant and tries to exploit Escape if at all possible. Escape counters with guile and boldness to protect its self-interest. This uneasy relationship works as long as there is genuine common interest.

You are in a weak position, though you really deserve better. You should use your initiative to improve things. The traditional text uses the image of a poor but intelligent girl who becomes a rich man's mistress. Providing both partners gain from the relationship, all goes well, but if the demands of the stronger become excessive, the weaker should leave. Being vulnerable, you are excused if the methods you use aren't quite ethical. Don't let yourself be put down.

Path 3.8/1 ☺

Lame but walking.
Tired and alone.
You win a great victory.

The image is of a person of limited means who must look after themselves as best they can. You will receive little help and in a tight corner you must be prepared to use unorthodox methods. You have to do what you have to do. Forceful progress can be successful in the short term. Even at a considerable disadvantage, you can win a contest. Use your cunning as well as force and don't let your guard down. Fight dirty if someone pushes you too far. Although this Path can overcome great obstacles, its luck will run out in time. For example, it's good for passing exams, but not so good for a career.

TIME: *Generally positive, you get your way even though you are at a disadvantage. A temporary or seasonal project will have a good run and may lead to something more permanent. A bit of sweat and struggle will do you good.*

Path 3.8/2 ☺

One-eyed, but able to see
Manages alone.
From sadness comes success.

You can't count on much help from other people, but being let down makes you resourceful and you do better on your own. Provided you are aware of your weaknesses they will not hamper you too badly, and cunning will help you to succeed. In this context, being 'one-eyed' is quite complimentary, the I Ching considers most humans to be blind.
TIME: *You may find yourself having to deal with problems alone. Although this sounds bad, you will cope very well. A short-term project will be successful and may lead to something more lasting.*

Path 3.8/3 ☹

The weaker partner is little better
Than a slave
Do not suffer this for long.

You will receive much less than you are due on this Path. Any plan you have in mind is really beneath you, you should look for something better. There will be delay in all matters. A tempting offer is not what it seems.
TIME: *You are in unsatisfactory and rather demeaning circumstances. You must look for something better in the long run. There is no reason why you should put up with poor conditions for ever.*

Path 3.8/4 ☺

Delayed partnership.
At first the weaker partner is rejected
Then accepted somewhat grudgingly.
Could be better, could be worse.

Delays are possible. A poor start, but problems sort themselves out in due course, if you keep your cool. In the long run you'll have to make changes if you want lasting success. A relationship will always be uneasy. Avoid entering into expensive agreements. Avoid long-term commitments.

TIME: *Delays and hindrances are overcome in time. This is a temporary phase in your life, get by as best you can. Avoid long-term commitments.*

Path 3.8/5 ☺

**The King's mistress is more beautiful
than his bride.
At the wedding she hides behind a veil
To avoid the new Queen's hatred.
The moon that is nearly full is the
Most favourable.**

This is about concealing something from the envy of others and letting it develop quietly. Beware of upsetting someone inadvertently, they can do you more damage than you think. On this Path, hiding virtue and playing down strength protect you from harm. Such modesty is considered very favourable. The reference to the moon means that once your power has reached its maximum it starts to decline. The advice is, be like the moon that is nearly full and don't shine too brightly. This Path has great wisdom, learn it. Don't worry about appearances, it's your inner quality that counts.

TIME: *Only limited progress is possible now. Don't fight with the authorities. Play your cards carefully and you could set yourself up with something better in the long run.*

Path 3.8/6 ☹

**At the wedding feast
The bride brings a basket with no
Fruit in it.
The groom sacrifices a sheep that
Doesn't bleed.**

There is nothing to be gained. Don't act. This old commentary is almost certainly a colourful way of saying that the wife is barren and the husband impotent. No good will come of it.

TIME: *Think about taking a new direction in life; the way things are, there's not much hope. Be active and take measures against the misfortune that's on its way.*

4. The House of Good Hunting

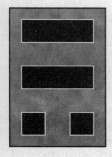

Seize the moment, follow your heart.
Be like the wind that goes everywhere.
Learn the secrets of the four corners
And penetrate the Dragon's treasure chest.
Act boldly, for indecision will lead to failure.

The House of Good Hunting is in many ways the most favourable house. The hunting technique can be applied to most things: money, love, study or spiritual growth. Good Hunting correlates to wind and like wind it can usually find what it wants. In this House you should be active and search for useful options. When you have spied out the land you can act. One of the reasons for Good Hunting's success is the variety of tactics that it uses. It can be subtle and penetrating or strong and forceful with all graduations in between.

The weaknesses to watch out for are indecision and impatience. The restless wind sees many fascinating things and can never settle down.

Situation 4.1 Small Gains

**Small success.
Dense clouds but no rain.
The home is safe.**

*Challenge in the House of Good Hunting. No real harmony here.
Good Hunting finds the authoritarian Challenge an unwelcome guest
and keeps out of its way. Provided there are no commitments
arguments will come to nothing.*

'Dense clouds but no rain' means either an apparently imminent
crisis that never actually happens, or promised benefits that never
materialize. This Situation is never more than adequate and
nothing of significance can be achieved.

Path 4.1/1 ☺

**Small gains in safety.
Then returning home brings good
Fortune.**

Often it turns out that what you have in mind is not really essential
and is probably best postponed. Provided you do not expect much
you can follow this Path in safety. Small matters go well, but
important issues should be avoided.

TIME: *A very safe and generally pleasant time if you content yourself with minor
matters.*

Path 4.1/2 ☺

**Persuaded to return.
Small gains in continuing.
No cause for regret.**

Avoid commitments even if it is very tempting to make them. You
must 'persuade' yourself to stick to small things, which will go well.

TIME: *Safe enough, but nothing of import should be undertaken. Avoid grand schemes.*

Path 4.1/3 ☹

An apparent victory.
Much to lose.
The axle breaks,
Husband and wife roll their eyes.

There is some possibility of loss on this Path, better not to act at present.

TIME: *All kinds of aggravation must be borne with good grace. Avoid quarrels. Remember who your real friends are.*

Path 4.1/4 ☹

Much to lose.
Pushing ahead may lead to bloodshed.
It is still easy to withdraw.

'Bloodshed' is probably something of an exaggeration. What it generally means is that you may be tempted to make a foolish mistake. However, even at the last minute it is not too late to withdraw and save yourself the humiliation of failure.

TIME: *Keep out of trouble. Don't back people into corners, they will turn nasty. Quietly getting on with life is good. Not good for grand schemes.*

Path 4.1/5 ☺

Small gains with a friend.

Good for any minor project. A deep friendship or romance will come to nothing, but casual friendship can be pleasant.

TIME: *Small matters go well and generally life is quite pleasant. Expect no more and all will go well.*

Path 4.1/6 ☹

> Rain starts and stops fitfully.
> Many small gains.
> A woman continues quietly,
> A man tries to push ahead.
> Both fail.
> Beware the fall of the moon.
> The demands of fate keep changing.

In theory, by making small gains over a long period of time it is possible to build something great. However, it only takes one mistake to wreck months of work, and this is what often happens on this Path. Provided you expect very little you can continue in safety. A new project will be more trouble than it's worth.

TIME: *Worrying, something you have worked on for a long time can be ruined by a silly mistake. Protect your interests carefully.*

Situation 4.2 Over the Horizon

**After washing the hands
A pause.
The ceremony is yet to begin.**

*Development (flat earth) in the House of Good Hunting (wind).
Wind travels well over flat earth, and from a height a great
distance can be seen.*

This Situation is about seeing your life in the long term. If your view
of life is too narrow, there is a danger that what is really important
for the future is being neglected. Petty issues can easily dominate
one's thoughts. Before going further it's good to take a break to see
things from an impartial point of view. It may be that a new start or
another location is favourable. Then again, it may just be your
attitude that needs altering. Look back at your life. What has gone
well? What has gone badly? Why? Don't concern yourself with
principles of right and wrong or where to place the blame. Look at
the results of your actions and those of others. Think hard about
what has brought happiness and how to repeat it. Think hard about
what has brought sorrow and how to avoid it. This Situation is
about a state of mind that you should always cultivate, nothing is so
certain that it should never be questioned. This doesn't mean
getting involved in endless indecision or self-doubt, just take a
moment to think before acting. Travel and study are favourable.

Path 4.2/1 ☺

**Immature outlook.
You must broaden your view.
Those who do not compete will never lose.
The strong will suffer.**

You are probably being naive in your expectations. A scheme will not
work out the way you planned it. Usually a strong person who makes a
good effort can expect success, but here a weak person who doesn't even
try does better, because they will be spared the ignominy of failure.

TIME: *Trivial problems make it hard to see ahead. Do the best you can to keep on course. A person in a responsible position is likely to suffer during this time. Failure to make good decisions matters more if others rely on you.*

Path 4.2/2 ☹

Narrow view
Like that of an old-fashioned
Housewife.
This is only good in a weak person.

You are in a weak position. You need to think again about any plans you make. What are the long-term effects likely to be?

TIME: *It is sometimes hard to see the wood for the trees. Take a generous attitude towards the failings of others, a housewife's view implies bigotry. If you are in a responsible position you are likely to suffer if your judgement is poor.*

Path 4.2/3 ☺

Whether advancing or retreating
It is better to act decisively.

Dithering will make it difficult for you to advance or retreat. Assess the situation and make a decision quickly.

TIME: *Don't allow yourself to procrastinate, face important decisions with courage.*

Path 4.2/4 ☺☺

Seeing the glory of the kingdom
In touch with the ruler.
All goes well.

To 'see the glory' is to know what is best for all concerned. People in authority can be approached. Travel and moving are very favourable.

TIME: *Generally good, you can make changes, go on holiday or move.*

Path 4.2/5 ☺

Watching one's own actions
There is much to learn.

Look at the results of what you have done in the past and judge how successful you have been. Give thought to your effect on other people. Then act with confidence.

TIME: *A good time to move, or start something new.*

Path 4.2/6 ☺☺

Looking down from the heights
Everything is clear.
No mistake is made.

Very lucky, especially for long-term changes, you will benefit spiritually as well as materially. You know what needs to be done and should act. 'The heights' means both a good view and high principles.

TIME: *This is a very good omen, particularly if you are moving or otherwise making important changes. Good for travel, moving or putting new plans into effect.*

Situation 4.3 Rise to the Challenge

Change is needed.
Follow your heart and seize the moment.
The centre is moved.
Those who ride the storm are glad indeed.
Those who stay behind suffer misfortune.

Awakening (thunder) in the House of Good Hunting (wind).
Unstable, but dynamic and high in achievement.

This Situation encourages you to go beyond your usual limits, in fact the advice often seems absurdly over-ambitious. However, in my experience it always turns out to be well within the limits of your abilities and the rewards are great.

There is a need for a major change, but what should that change be? This can be difficult to establish and a certain amount of trial and error is to be expected. The important thing is to get moving while you can. In this Situation it is all too easy to let the moment pass, which is a mistake you will live to regret. It is usually easy to see what should have been done after it is too late.

At the moment your position is quite strong, but time is against you, use your power now, soon it will be too late. If you do act there is much to gain, so be brave, cast caution to the wind and follow your heart. Then the storm will carry you safely beyond all danger.

The changes you make will lead you closer to your true self. The true self contains your natural affinities, the people, activities and places closest to your heart. Your life at present is not allowing you to express this nature, which is why you must change. Be warned, this may not be easy.

Path 4.3/1 ☺☺

Accept the challenge.
Ride the storm.
Do great things.

Follow this Path with sufficient determination and you will win great rewards. Be decisive, take advantage of any opportunity.

TIME: *Problems arise that show grave weakness in your way of life. To continue without making changes is dangerous. Decisive action now will reshape your life for the better.*

Path 4.3/2 ☺☺

> **Great changes.**
> **Ten tortoises give their blessing.**
> **True intentions.**
> **No mistakes.**

Great efforts are needed to overcome great obstacles. Tortoises were used in divination, so this means ten favourable forecasts, in other words very lucky indeed. This doesn't mean that it'll be easy.

TIME: *Great changes are needed and if you have the courage to make them, great success will be yours. If you fail to act positively you will regret it.*

Path 4.3/3 ☺

> **Unwelcome changes bring good fortune.**
> **Carry a jade tablet**
> **Then even nobles will obey.**

In times of trouble the normal rules break down. When ill, even a prince must take the advice of a doctor. The 'jade tablet' is a symbol of authority, this means that you have power enough to do what needs doing and others will not stand in your way.

TIME: *Difficult times, but if you ride the storm you will find good fortune.*

Path 4.3/4 ☺☺

> **Moving the centre**
> **Walk in the middle.**
> **Check your authority**
> **Even nobles obey.**
> **Good fortune.**

This is a powerful Path. 'Moving the centre' means changing something fundamental. Authority cannot be taken for granted in important matters, check that you are acting in the best interest of all. 'Walking in the middle' means making necessary compromises.

TIME: *This may not seem a very favourable time as change is often painful and knowing what changes are needed takes a lot of heart-searching. Summon up courage in your convictions and do what you know in your heart must be done, then you will win a great victory for yourself.*

Path 4.3/5 ☺☺

Sincere and generous.
Faithful and dedicated.
No need to ask.

The advice here is about how to maintain success rather than acquire it. If you cultivate the good qualities mentioned, there will be little need to consult oracles as your fortune will always be good. In practical terms any plan that is put into effect vigorously will bring great success. This is why it's worth thinking about how to deal with success when you have attained it.

TIME: *Change is never easy, but here it can be made successfully. Seize the moment and change your fate for the better.*

Path 4.3/6 ☹

Go no further.
Envious ones will strike you.
Make the base broader.
Keep the enemy happy.

Here a success leads you into danger, sinister forces gather round you, a plan must be devised to counter their influence. 'Broadening the base' means making sure many people benefit from your existence. 'Keeping the enemy happy' means paying off trouble for the time being.

TIME: *You will have to be very cunning if you are to avoid injury. Avoid unsettling people at all costs.*

Situation 4.4 Opportunity

**Three types of game to hunt.
Stalk like a gentle breeze**

Run like the wind to bring the prey down.

*Good Hunting in the House of Good Hunting. This is a very
harmonious and potentially productive relationship; make the most of it.*

A hunter watches, assesses, then steals up on the prey gently. When
the final move is made, it's so fast and sure that there can be only one
outcome. From this example we learn to combine knowledge with
action. If you are gentle the truth will not be hidden from you and to
know the truth gives you the power to act effectively.

In terms of strategy, a problem should first be dissected and
broken into smaller units. These small units can be picked off, one by
one. In a hunting party each member has a specific task, through co-
ordinated effort hunters armed only with spears could bring down
the most dangerous prey.

You often get this Situation when you face a difficult but
worthwhile task. First you must be cautious and weigh up where
your interests lie, then make your move. You are warned not to
allow caution to become weakness. Act quickly, firmly and follow
through with determination, then success will come. This Situation
teaches us how to use our intelligence to spy out the land, analyse the
situation, then develop a plan of action to put it into practice.

Path 4.4/1 ☺

**Commitment wavers.
Advance or retreat?
Press on like a warrior
Doubts will disappear.**

There is cause for doubt, but it usually proves to be unfounded. You may well suffer some soul-searching over this one, but if you examine the issue carefully then act with confidence, all will go well.

TIME: *You will be assailed by doubts that will turn out to be largely unfounded. This is a time to push yourself and do all the things you've been meaning to do. It is important that you act decisively, or it will be all too easy to lose your direction. Sometimes it's better to be wrong than indecisive.*

Path 4.4/2 ☺

Unexpected opportunity.
One thing leads to another.
The wind goes everywhere.
Even under the bed.

Good for most matters. Often doing something relatively trivial causes you to see life in a new light and may lead to an important move. This happens in an unexpected way. Be bold, but aware of your best interests. Look very carefully into other people's motives, all may not be as it seems.

TIME: *You must look carefully at your situation and then act clearly. If you are indecisive you will achieve nothing, if you are rash you'll run into trouble.*

Path 4.4/3 ☹

Wavering commitment,
Too many attempts.
Become determined and succeed.

It is no good spending your time going over your options again and again. Life is tough, you must get on with it, once you've overcome your reluctance you'll feel better. Even if the project you are involved in doesn't turn out brilliantly, provided you've put in a good effort you'll be better placed to succeed next time.

TIME: *Doubts and fears are largely unfounded, don't let them put you off your course. This is a time when lots of petty problems mount up and seem serious, but if you press on regardless they will get sorted out one way or another.*

Path 4.4/4 ☺

Three kinds of game.
Deeply committed.
Act like a hunter.

The 'three kinds of game' are adventure, power (wealth) and knowledge. This Path often refers to learning something very valuable in the long run, but it can be a pretty hard path to follow through. It may be that you cannot achieve all you would like to, but it is well worth trying, as the lessons you learn will stand you in good stead.

TIME: *Not necessarily easy, but good effort will win excellent rewards; make the most of opportunities at this time. Travel or starting something new should be considered.*

Path 4.4/5 ☺

A poor start, but a good end.
Prepare for three days.
Be careful for three days after.

The outlook is difficult at first, but good in the long term.

TIME: *Keep working steadily even though the going is tough, and your position will improve greatly. Travel and new projects go well.*

Path 4.4/6 ☹

Mislays property and an axe.
Finish commitments.

An axe is both a tool and a means of defence, so 'mislaying' it (I say mislay because in my experience this is a temporary problem) exposes one to danger. In modern times this could refer to a mechanical breakdown. Sixth Paths often mean that it's necessary to complete one thing before going on to another and that moving ahead too fast exposes one to danger.

TIME: *Tie up loose ends and bring your affairs to completion. A time to be firm with yourself.*

Situation 4.5 Moving

Time to leave.
Sail on the next tide.
To obtain the blessing of the ancestors
Kings of old offered sacrifice at the temple
Knowing it is greater to give than receive.

Danger (water, moon) in the House of Good Hunting (wind, wood). Wind blows steady over water, and boats were made of wood. These archetypes like to travel and disperse themselves, so money is hard to hold on to. However this Situation is also associated with the sowing of grain, which means that spending now will bring rewards in the future. A kind deed nourishes the seed of spiritual growth.

One cannot remain static forever and now you have the opportunity to move. This must be done while the going is good, because failure to act will leave you in an unfortunate position. There should be no undue haste, however, moving is not the same thing as taking flight. Spend as much time as you require to make plans and enquiries, then leave when the time is right. Sometimes several adjustments have to be made before the final destination becomes clear. There is a danger here that in the process of planning you will lose your momentum and lose the moment, but this would be a shame. Keep your mind fixed on your goal.

Path 4.5/1 ☺

A good horse gives all its strength.

A good omen, use all your strength and you will succeed. By helping others you'll help yourself. Travel is favoured. If you miss your chance you'll regret it.

TIME: *Make changes, be bold, there is much to be gained by using initiative. Use this favourable time to the full or face misfortune later.*

Path 4.5/2 ☺

Sailing with the tide
Take that which you need the most
Then there will be no regret.

Taking only what you need most often means difficult decisions over priorities. What is it that is most important to you? Once you've made your mind up about that, the rest of your plans will go smoothly.

TIME: *Look for opportunities to travel or begin new projects. Follow your heart rather than worldly wisdom.*

Path 4.5/3 ☹

Let go of your anchor and sail.
Action removes doubt.

Exploit opportunity, it's no good agonizing over decisions for too long. Set your course and be on your way.

TIME: *Keep yourself moving even if it is just running on the spot. Much uncertainty clears up if you act decisively. There is good fortune if you go beyond your usual limits.*

Path 4.5/4 ☺

Sailing away from your group.
Careful planning brings good fortune.
Spending now will bring returns later.

This is a good Path, but it needs careful thought to exploit it properly. In business you'll get a better deal from another supplier.

TIME: *A new start or some exciting project will be successful provided it is well planned.*

Path 4.5/5 ☺

Worried and sweating.
A cry of joy at leaving.
Sail away!
Live like a king without regret.

There may be some hitches here before you can be on your way, but when you do, it will all be worthwhile.

TIME: *Take the opportunities that fate offers. Good to travel or just get about more.*

Path 4.5/6 ☺☺

Dissolving the bonds of blood.
Crossing over the water.
Staying far away brings good fortune.

This is a great Path for travelling, or just about any plan. 'Bonds of blood' sounds scary, but I am pretty sure it is just something to do with leaving emotional baggage behind.

TIME: *Good to travel or start something new. Most matters go well.*

Situation 4.6 Home

Walk without fear
All the world is your home.
Passionate yet gentle
Everything finds its true place.

Intensity in the House of Good Hunting (ability). This is a perfect combination, Intensity knows what it wants, and Good Hunting knows how to get it. This convergence of interests lasts because there is genuine affinity in this relationship.

In this most favourable Situation everything finds its proper place and all disputes are resolved. Opportunities for advancement exist in spiritual, personal, and professional fields. The concept of 'home' here is very broad, more like a feeling of belonging and doing the right thing at the right time. It could involve things you have been involved with for years or something brand new. Sometimes one meets people for the first time and feels as if one had known them for years. The same is true of places and it's this feeling of inner affinity that gives you the strength to create good fortune for yourself and those around you. If your 'home' is where you have always been, you should remain there, but if your heart is somewhere else now is the time to go. Only you know where your true home lies, but wherever and whatever it is, you are going the right way.

Path 4.6/1 ☺☺

As safe as a babe in arms.
Wherever you go you are well looked after.

This is a good Path for anything you have in mind.
TIME: *Promising. Make the most of this fortunate time and set your life on a better footing. Anything you make a sincere effort at will succeed.*

Path 4.6/2 ☺☺

**Like a noble's child
Guided and helped,
At home wherever you go.**

An opportunity not to be missed. Once on this Path you can just go with the flow. Everything will work out nicely.

TIME: *A very good time for most matters; make the most of it.*

Path 4.6/3 ☺

**Don't hang around giggling like a child.
First learn discipline, then relax.
If quarrels come, defending the indefensible makes
you ridiculous.
Be active and helpful then all will go well.**

This is essentially a mild rebuke. In favourable Situations there is a temptation to take things too easy. An attitude of 'if everything is OK why bother to try hard' can creep in. Of course if this is allowed to continue it will undermine the good fortune you enjoy.

TIME: *Good, make sure you get the full benefit from this time. Work hard and be helpful.*

Path 4.6/4 ☺☺

**One who serves the family well
Becomes the treasure of the house,
And must be kept safe.**

A good Path that can be followed with confidence. If you're steady, hard-working and kind you will always be respected. It's lucky to swallow your pride and do what others want. All matters go well, and business is good.

TIME: *The real treasure of the house is the willingness to work unselfishly for the common good. Be peaceful. Your work will win praise. Enjoy the company of new and old friends. Work and studies go well. Keep quiet about your ambitions for now.*

Path 4.6/5 ☺☺

A benign monarch
Rules with love
Sets a fine example.
A little firmness is required.

Very favourable for any endeavour, move ahead with confidence. Setting a good example works better than making people fear you. You have an important function in your group. Exert your authority gently. All goes well.

TIME: *Very good. See friends and family. Business and studies go well. Work hard to extract the maximum benefit.*

Path 4.6/6 ☺☺

The clan extends its territory.
When you do what you do well,
You are worthy of respect.
Success will come to you.

Now you have the power to do something ambitious, move ahead with confidence.

TIME: *Very positive. Enjoy the company of friends and relations. A great work can be accomplished. Very good for working for your future.*

Situation 4.7. Disappointment

 A wild goose that flies alone through the wilderness
Has no one to depend on.
Not as you hoped.
The path is often obstructed.
Little danger, but many disappointments.
The cause must be great to warrant this.

Firm Purpose in the House of Good Hunting. Although friendly, there is little to hold these two together, Good Hunting follows the breeze and Firm Purpose sits still as a mountain.

Don't have high expectations and you won't be disappointed. A goose is a gregarious bird and if it flies alone it means it has lost its companions. This is not a Situation one would choose, but if you go in with your eyes open there is no real danger. Things often just don't work out how you would have liked and you are left with a feeling of lost potential. Although you can survive and even improve your position it will be hard and there will be a sense of sadness that things should be so difficult.

Path 4.7/1 ☹

The wild goose leaves the lake.
A young one seeks a living.
Better to walk alone than with those who would harm you.

You have a good attitude and ability, but are alone in a fairly negative world. People accept you only grudgingly and may plot against you. Your best bet is not to rely on anyone and just look after your own interests. There are few potential gains and many potential losses on this Path. A purchase will prove a disappointment.

TIME: *A difficult time, things you are involved in are likely to fail, or perform poorly. However, studies and things that you are in sole charge of will go well. It might be better to retreat while considering a change of direction. If your heart is set on continuing, be very careful and things may work out well in the end. In a confrontation you will come off the worst.*

Path 4.7/2 ☺

The wild goose reaches the land.
It finds food for the long journey.
It calls to its comrades.
There is no answer.

You have something good, but no one to share it with. You must continue alone. A purchase will prove a disappointment.
TIME: *You have enough, but are lonely. Be self-reliant and set things up for the future.*

Path 4.7/3 ☹

The wild goose reaches the desert.
A man goes hunting, but doesn't return.
A pregnant woman has no child.
Be prepared to defend yourself.

This is a very miserable Path. Whether you are active or passive you can achieve nothing. What little you have is under threat and must be fought for.
TIME: *Very poor times. Conserve your energies, you'll face many perils. To attain anything will be extremely difficult. Beware of thieves and slanderers.*

Path 4.7/4 ☺

The wild goose is in danger.
The trees are safe, if only there is a
Flat branch.

Any port in a storm. In a dangerous situation you sometimes have to do something against your nature (geese don't perch in trees). Anything you do will be a disappointment.
TIME: *Uncomfortable and possibly dangerous, you will have to do things you dislike.*

Path 4.7/5 ☺

Help is found, a good start,
Then disappointment.
A woman has no children for three
Years
Then she has many.

This is a stop-start Path. You wish to do something, you find help, but are let down. This process continues, but in the end there may be a good result. Accept what help you can get, without great expectation.

TIME: *You are just getting established in your way of life, you will have many troubles, but as long as you stay true to yourself you'll have success in the end. There may be sadness and loss.*

Path 4.7/6 ☺

Rejected and disappointed
The wild goose flies into the clouds.
Its feathers could be used in the
Sacred dance.
Fools do not know this.
Years later there is good fortune.

Continue your work alone. The world won't appreciate your worth for some time. Turn to spiritual development, or perhaps take a holiday. There is no danger, but there are delays.

TIME: *Difficulties you thought you had overcome reappear to make your life difficult. You can only improve your position slowly. Good spiritually, a pilgrimage may be helpful.*

Situation 4.8 Realization

**The invisible wind blows across the lake
Its secret nature apparent in a million
sparkling ripples.
The hidden power of fate is manifest in the
actions of living things.
Even pigs and fishes heed its call.
Good fortune.**

*Escape in the House of Good Hunting. The affinity between these
archetypes is profound.*

What makes one person love another? Why do they wish to live in
one place or have a particular career? These matters are governed
by their inner nature. When what you do reflects your inner self, you
have great power and are able to fulfil your destiny. In this Situation
the veil is lifted a little and truth can be glimpsed. If your life does
not conform to your true self it must be changed; if it does, this must
be encouraged. Study yourself and those around you carefully and
these truths may become clearer. Don't worry if you find this hard to
apply in life, it's a matter of allowing something to happen rather
than using force. In practice, if you let things develop in their own
way at their own pace then the inner forces work with or without
your conscious understanding.

This is a very spiritual Situation, the advice is to let the power of
the spirit guide you in your actions. When this happens danger is
overcome and rewards won. Romance and adventure are vital to
understanding this Situation, for love is the greatest motivator of
humans. If romance is harnessed to spiritual development then
literally anything is possible.

This is one of the Situations in which the I Ching speaks directly
and explains its attitude to you. The commentary on the second
Path is the I Ching's promise to the sincere practitioner.

Path 4.8/1 ☺

Be prepared for the unexpected.
Secret designs are unhelpful.

Keep a watchful eye, but make no plans, there are things you don't know. Behave in an open, but reserved way: secret deals and schemes should be avoided. If you're careful, success is possible.

TIME: *Think about the meaning of your life. What do you feel really wholehearted about? If that's what you're doing, keep hard at it, if not, it's time you returned to your true nature.*

Path 4.8/2 ☺☺

Gentle attraction.
A crane calls softly to its young.
Come, I will guard you with my shadow.
There is fine wine in a gold goblet.
Heed the call that we may share it.

Mysterious attraction calls, be very quiet and a little voice will tell you what to do. Make no plans, everything must happen naturally. A sincere student will receive great rewards in due course. A break or holiday will be a meaningful experience. Love is very deep.

TIME: *To those who believe in what they are doing, continue and you will find the way to overcome all obstacles. To those who do not, now is the time to get out before it is too late. It's not enough to pursue material reward, if your heart isn't in it there will be no lasting success. A new romance is very possible.*

Path 4.8/3 ☹

Unequal attraction.
Follow your heart? Follow your head?
Only you can choose.
Friends beat the drum and sing,
Then stop and sob.

Assessing this Path is very difficult, there is a strong affinity between you and the object of the question. However it's an unstable affair bringing sorrow (sobbing) as well joy (singing and playing drums). This Path is often associated with romantic love, and although the feelings are deep, the relationship will be up-and-down.

TIME: *A time of difficult learning experiences. One minute things look good, the next you're in trouble. Do what you wish to, but be aware of the consequences. Studies go very well.*

Path 4.8/4 ☺☺

Adventure calls.
A fine horse escapes from the stable.
Be as the moon nearly full
Then all your hunting will be rewarded.

If you have the chance, escape from the humdrum and do something exciting, do it now. You can take big risks because the mysterious power aids you. The moon is strongest just before it is full, for fullness is the beginning of decline. The young are flexible as well as strong. To remain youthful, you must turn away from the dreary repetition of ordinary life and seek more imaginative ways of using your time.

TIME: *Be true to yourself and you can attempt anything.*

Path 4.8/5 ☺☺

Inner attraction,
Secret truth is made known.
The invisible links are seen.

The reason for a difficulty can be found and the steps taken to clear the problem. Anything of a spiritual or uplifting nature will go very well. Good for seeing people and going places, useful contacts can be made. A sincere student will make a genuine contribution to human wisdom. A break or holiday will be a meaningful experience. Love is very deep.

TIME: *The meaning of your life becomes clearer; there may be sadness, but in the end the truth will lead you to a better way. If you feel you are on your true path you should continue with great vigour, if not, now you have a chance to break with the past and strike out anew. Now it is good to improve human relations and work hard at studies.*

Path 4.8/6 ☺

A cock's call cannot reach heaven.
Flying high will lead to a fall.

There is a danger of impatience leading you astray, Path six often means that matters must be completed properly.

TIME: *A time of restlessness. You may get flashes of insight, and be tempted to behave rashly, but it's not yet time to be bold. Get on with your ordinary tasks and look after your family. Now it is good to improve human relations and work hard at studies.*

5. The House of Adversity

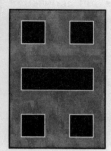

The path to success leads
through the valley of
adversity.
Fools who blunder ahead will
suffer.
When in danger take the line
Of least resistance.
There is no ravine that water
cannot escape from.

In the House of Adversity life is a bit harder than in the other Houses. This doesn't mean that disaster is inevitable, or success unobtainable, merely that a respectful approach is needed. It is no place for fools, whose weaknesses will be exposed mercilessly.

It is important to remember that all beings must cross the Valley of Adversity from time to time. Some don't make it and this makes it easier for the ones who are left. Those who learn to deal with Adversity effectively are at a great advantage in the struggle of life.

This House is associated with water and its dangers. Water easily runs away, so loss is possible, not good for business. Water is unpredictable, one moment calm, next raging, so prepare for storms.

On the plus side, water is very good at escaping, so copy its example and always take the path of least resistance. Water is also very patient, it slowly fills up a pit until it can flow away.

Being in this House can be compared to sailing in a flimsy boat on choppy waters. The force of the elements can tear you apart at any second, yet by having respect for and knowledge of the risks a voyage can be successfully completed.

The House of Adversity is particularly good for students, the sincere and the profound.

Situation 5.1 Prepare

Waiting on the sand.
There is food, drink and time to spare.
Build your strength.
When the boat is ready, cross the great
water.

Challenge in the House of Adversity. Challenge has great patience
and determination, it can escape all Adversity's pitfalls.

This is not an ideal Situation, but this shouldn't discourage you. The
image is of waiting by water to cross it. There's work to do on the
boat before the crossing can be made. This delay can be used to
advantage to get fit and relaxed before taking to sea.

There are two dangers here. The first is that one becomes lazy and
neglects essential work. The second comes from impatient hurrying
that lacks thoroughness. Both these attitudes lead to failure.

The correct approach is measured and steady, dealing with each
problem thoughtfully and thoroughly. When preparations are made
in this way, great things can be accomplished. Study and training
are well favoured. Money is hard to come by and business slow,
avoid making any investments. For a student, knuckling down to
work will bring great success.

Path 5.1/1 ☺

Held in a meadow.
Plenty of time to prepare.

The meadow is quite a good place to prepare and therefore there is
no need to rush ahead. Postpone or abandon plans. Keep your mind
on your purpose and use the time.

TIME: *Waiting for change is always difficult. The best thing to do is take life*
easy, working quietly and enjoying the simple pleasures of life. Be patient, your
time will come.

Path 5.1/2 ☺

On an uncomfortable riverbank.
Grumbling.
Hold fast and all will go well.

You are in a tiresome position, but trying to change things will only make it worse. You'll just have to knuckle down for the moment and work on turning your dreams into realities later.

TIME: *An irritating time; just make the best of it, better times will come. Health and business interests may suffer if you're not careful.*

Path 5.1/3 ☹

Stuck in the mud.
Too far too quickly.
Grit and determination.

You are in a bad situation to prepare. This Path often means that you have started something prematurely and got stuck. Keep steady and don't take on anything new, concentrate on getting yourself out of trouble.

TIME: *Tiresome and difficult times. The only thing to do is continue working steadily and quietly until you get out of trouble.*

Path 5.1/4 ☹

The water goes over your head.
Things are very uncomfortable.
Continue with great care.
Things improve in time.

This is not a Path to choose. Often it refers to something that has started badly and it's difficult to know whether to continue. Having the water go over your head means that matters go beyond your control. There is a danger of panic leading you into real trouble. Do what you can to alleviate discomfort.

TIME: *This an unhappy time, it's very hard to know whether to keep going or retreat. Quite a lot of manœuvring is necessary to extricate yourself from trouble.*

Path 5.1/5 ☺

Preparing in pleasant circumstances.
Eat, drink and relax.

This is the best of the Paths in this Situation, for it allows you to observe things from a comfortable position. Rest up and wait for the time to act.

TIME: *A pleasant time, provided you don't become impatient. Take things easy and enjoy the simple pleasures of life.*

Path 5.1/6 ☹

Waiting in a cave.
Three people arrive.
They will show you the way.

The disadvantage of waiting in a cave is you can't see what's going on. 'Three people arriving' means a sign will come when it's time to leave.

TIME: *Tiresome and difficult times. This often refers to being stuck in a rut. There is no use giving way to impatience, a sign will come in due course.*

Situation 5.2 Take the Initiative

You can succeed.
There are obstacles and dangers.
Concentrate on the immediate future.
Show unwavering allegiance.
Those who delay get nothing.
Consult the *Guide* again as matters develop.

Development in the House of Adversity doesn't sound all that good,
but in practice these two get on well and form an effective team.

This is the only really favourable Situation in the House of Adversity
and represents the easiest way out of danger. Generally in this House
bold action leads to failure, but here a quick move leaves trouble
behind.

As well as overcoming problems you can make gains from taking
risks at this time. Team work will succeed even if there is tension. Don't
let yourself become isolated by being seen to be negative or tardy.

Path 5.2/1 ☺☺

A bowl of good food.
Have faith and take the initiative.
Danger is left behind.

Not only can you escape danger, but there are unexpected gains.
Don't be shy about taking what comes your way.
TIME: *Very positive. If you're in trouble, you can free yourself. Be bold, fate*
favours you.

Path 5.2/2 ☺☺

Seize the initiative.
Keep your inner balance.
A call receives a response.

Good for most things. On this Path danger is left behind by resolute
action. Calculate the risks and act.

TIME: *A good time for freeing yourself from old problems and moving on to fresh challenges.*

Path 5.2/3 ☺

Even difficult people are open to reason.
There is danger.
You can succeed.

Success, in spite of problems. A dangerous venture can be undertaken. Act firmly, but with caution.

TIME: *Generally good. Some upheavals and trouble with people. If you are thoughtful in your actions, there's nothing to worry about.*

Path 5.2/4 ☺

When the time is right
Take the initiative.
Look outward.

Fourth Paths often suffer some delay, so don't worry if things don't happen quite according to plan. This is basically a good Path and you should follow it with confidence.

TIME: *Act boldly and look for ways to improve your life. You can make progress in your business and studies and even find time to enjoy time off with friends.*

Path 5.2/5 ☺

The hunt draws to an end.
Take the reward you have earned.
Treat danger with respect.

Even dangerous things are possible, if you are careful. There will be set-backs, but success is sweet. This Path is sometimes the last part of an era.

TIME: *Times may seem tough, but a series of calculated risks will pay off. A somewhat martial attitude is favourable.*

Path 5.2/6 ☹☹

Troubles mount.
The head lost.
Understandable, but no way to behave.

Here we find a strong temptation to abandon one's path and do something silly. Often something that seems a good idea turns out to be a matter of considerable regret in the long run. This Path is to be avoided. If you're planning something, abandon it, you have other duties to attend to. Continuing will destroy what you have.

TIME: *Even though your faith may be sorely tested you should continue with existing plans. Generally, you get this Path when you're about to give something up because it seems too much trouble, but this will prove a bad mistake, so don't do it.*

Situation 5.3 Somehow

You can succeed
With effort, and intelligence.
Take what help you can find.
Do not take on anything new.

Awakening (thunder) in the House of Adversity (rain). A stormy,
wet ride, these two get into all kinds of trouble.

This is not a Situation one would choose to be in, conditions are
difficult and success uncertain. Some kind of transition is needed.
There are problems ahead, you need push and initiative, but it is
most important that you are flexible. Get the feel of the Situation
and use your instincts. When you have decided what to do, think
about the easiest and safest way to do it. The Paths tell you when to
try harder and when to back off. Concentrate on clearing existing
obstacles before undertaking anything new.

Path 5.3/1 ☺

Many difficulties making a transition.
Look for help.
Finish what you have started.

Take what measures are needed and any help you can get. Once you
are over immediate problems, life will look much better.
TIME: *There are many problems to sort out, if you set to work with energy and*
intelligence all will go well. Don't worry if you can't do things as well as you
would like; be happy just to lay the framework, you can improve the detail later.

Path 5.3/2 ☺

Horse and wagon part.
A temporary parting of the ways.
After ten units of time, begin-again.

Progress is obstructed and there is little that can be done for now.
TIME: *Do not give up your plans even though you may not be able to make*

much progress for a while. Take a diversion and come back when things are better.

Path 5.3/3 ☹☹

Dangerous country without a guide.
No opportunity, look to your safety.

Serious trouble, get out while the going is good. Do not be deceived. If you have to see things through you will need to pull every trick in the book to keep out of trouble. Look for any help available and don't hesitate to make use of it.

TIME: *If things can go wrong they will! Avoid doing things where possible. It might be time to retire, take a new direction in life or spend more time with your family.*

Path 5.3/4 ☺

Horse and wagon part.
Seek help without shame.
Things will work out in the end.

Life gets difficult, just hold on for the time being. It is best to continue quietly sorting minor matters.

TIME: *There are many problems that you would like to tackle, but now is not the time. Get minor problems out of the way while you wait.*

Path 5.3/5 ☺

Last-minute problems.
Handle delicately.
Don't jeopardize your hard work.

Improvement is coming, keep steady. It's possible to make progress even on difficult matters, but be careful.

TIME: *Not that bad, but a bit too much effort to be any real fun. Things you've been working at can be successfully completed. You may be tempted to get into trouble, an offer may not be what it seems. Avoid arguments.*

Path 5.3/6 ☹

**Horse and wagon part
Fed up with endless difficulties.
Give up now and you will cry later.
Try harder and things soon get better.**

This Path is an unnecessary diversion and should not be followed if possible. Stick with what you are already doing and don't throw in the towel. Things may look bad, but the fight will turn in your favour if you hang on. If it all gets too much, take a break, but don't make any rash decisions while you're tired and depressed. Don't take on anything new.

TIME: *You will find yourself restless and dissatisfied. If you give way to this you may lose something that you value little at the moment, but will be very sorry when it has gone. Impatience and lack of forethought cause you to miss an important meeting.*

Situation 5.4 The Water of Life

**Even if the buildings are fine,
A town cannot prosper without a well.
A good well gives water every year.
A well that is shallow cannot be relied upon.
A well that is dirty gives bad water.
If the rope breaks, no water can be drawn.
Only when the well is serviced can the
water be used.**

*Good Hunting (wood) in the House of Adversity (water). Wood
(bucket) under water means a well.*

This is often quite difficult to interpret. What the *Guide* is doing is
asking you to look at your lifestyle and motives carefully. What is it
that is essential to your survival and happiness? This is what
metaphorically could be called the 'water of life'. The commentary
gives you a rule of thumb to judge yourself by. The 'town with fine
buildings but no well' represents someone with wealth but no
happiness. The 'shallow well' refers to someone who is always
trying different things, but never putting in enough effort to get
a good result. The 'dirty well' is like a person who lets their good
qualities go to waste through negligence.

This is not a good Situation for doing things, it's time to take stock
of your life. Good fortune will come when you have understood and
exploited your best qualities.

Path 5.4/1 ☹

**Neglected well.
The water has clouded.
Not even fit for animals.**

You're not in good shape and following this Path leads to misfortune.
TIME: *Nothing's going well, you're very stale and need to make changes – but
don't proceed rashly. Take time off and think of how to make lasting
improvements to your life.*

Path 5.4/2 ☹☹

If the rope snaps, the jug will break.
Without a jug the well is only good for catching minnows.

Danger of accident or misfortune of some kind, best avoid this Path.

TIME: *Carelessness makes a difficult time worse, be on your guard. The less you attempt at this time the better. Some fundamental changes are needed to avoid troubles in the future, and now is the time to think about making them. You can put them into practice at a more favourable time.*

Path 5.4/3 ☺

The well has good water, but no one drinks.
My heart is sad.
So many are thirsty,
Yet the King does nothing.

On a practical level, this probably isn't a particularly useful Path. You aren't in a position to enjoy the use of your talents.

TIME: *Your talents are being wasted at present and the I Ching expresses its sympathy. However there is nothing to be done at present except continue quietly and make plans for the future.*

Path 5.4/4 ☺

The well is being repaired.
It cannot be used now.
Soon all will benefit.

Some kind of fundamental restructuring is taking place, let things be for now.

TIME: *Rest and recuperation. A good time to carry out repairs.*

Path 5.4/5 ☺

A clear cool spring.
You may drink.

The luck on this Path comes from repose, not action. Most business, travel and career plans will do badly, though studies, meditations and gatherings will go well. You often receive this oracle if you are about to become embroiled in troubles, but if you just keep still and don't take sides you'll escape harm.

TIME: *Good for quietly getting on with your life. Studies are favoured, business is slow. Think of your spiritual progress.*

Path 5.4/6 ☺

Plenty of water.
Take what you need.
It will not run dry.

The same as the last Path, but there seems to be even more water here. The luck on this Path comes from repose, not action. Most business, travel and career plans will do badly, though studies, meditations and gatherings may go very well. You often receive this oracle if you are about to become embroiled in troubles, but if you just keep still and don't take sides you will escape harm.

TIME: *A harmonious time, very good for study and meditation. Try to be quiet and thoughtful.*

Situation 5.5 Through the Dark Valley

**There are many pitfalls.
If your heart is in the right place.
Take the easiest road
and leave the danger behind.**

Adversity in the House of Adversity, not an ideal combination.

This is a dangerous Situation. Not only is it a time of mental and physical stress, but it is likely that under this pressure you will make mistakes that lead to serious consequences. One would not go this way by choice. If it can't be avoided, it's vital that you keep your nerve, set your heart on escape and use your intelligence to find the Path of least resistance. Those who have a good attitude have a very good chance of making it through safely.

Another meaning is to do with water quality of depth and purity. This means that studies and spiritual practices go very well. Often if one devotes oneself to such works the difficult time passes without mishap.

There is one other circumstance in which this Situation is favourable, that is for parties and gatherings; these can be riotously good, though there may be some mishaps.

Path 5.5/1 ☹

**Entering the dark valley.
Falling into a hole.
This should be avoided.**

To proceed will lead you into danger.

TIME: *Poor; look after your health and possessions very carefully. Do not make enemies, they may destroy you. Meditation and studies are favoured.*

Path 5.5/2 ☺

A path in the dark valley
Surrounded by pitfalls.
If you act hastily you will fall.
Pause and think how to extricate
Yourself.

Avoid this Path if possible. If you have some commitments that place you in danger, it is difficult but not impossible to escape.

TIME: *Danger surrounds you, but does not touch you if you keep yourself focused. If you're careful, this time will pass without great loss. Reduce commitments. Do not make enemies, they may destroy you. Studies and spiritual practices are extremely successful.*

Path 5.5/3 ☹

Lost in the dark valley
Quicksand in front and behind.
Take one step at a time.
If you fall, do not struggle,
You will only sink faster.

Avoid this Path if possible. The greatest caution is needed.

TIME: *Very tricky, you will have to take things very calmly if you want to extricate yourself. Reduce commitments to a minimum. Study and meditation will bring good fortune.*

Path 5.5/4 ☺

A window opens.
A jug of wine and bowl of rice.
Simple comforts sustain you in your
Trouble.

To advance now is not good, unless it is the best way out of a difficult situation. A timely compromise could get you out of trouble. If you sit back and relax danger will pass you by.

TIME: *Hard, but if you live simply you will come to no harm. Study and meditation will bring benefits.*

Path 5.5/5 ☺

The pits are filling with water.
Once they are full the water will flow
Out of the dark valley.

Like the water, you are about to escape the dark valley. Be patient,
you're not ready to act yet.

TIME: *You have been experiencing many hindrances, but soon the dark times will
be over. You must be careful not to be impetuous and not to undertake anything
until the danger is past.*

Path 5.5/6 ☹

Escape fails.
Tied up and imprisoned,
Impenetrable thorn bushes.
Kept in the dark for three years.

Here we have a continuation from the last Path(5.5/5), which finds
it fairly easy to wait until the time to act arrives. This Path (5.5/6) is
basically in the same position, but is more restless and is likely to
mess things up by trying to push ahead early.

TIME: *Sixth Paths tend to mean the end of something, in this case the darkness.
The danger here is that at the last moment one panics and makes a mistake that
leads to another 'three years' of suffering. Just keep steady and all will be well.*

Situation 5.6 The Old Fox

**Nearly across the frozen stream.
Be as wary as an old fox lest you slip on
the last yard.
On the other side there is game to hunt.
Soon you will be moving on again.**

*Intensity (fire) in the House of Adversity (water). Unstable, but
with plenty of chemistry, although Intensity may be damaged, as
water puts out fire.*

In this Situation something that appears reliable is in fact only
temporary. The image is of a frozen stream that behaves like solid
ground until the spring comes. There is still some time before the
thaw and you can still cross the stream safely if you are careful.

In practical terms this Situation means that what appears solid is
in fact delicately balanced. This means that a very delicate touch is
needed if nothing is to be upset.

Path 5.6/1 ☺

**Put on the brakes.
Then at worst it will be only the tail that gets wet.**

Even with the greatest care some mistakes are inevitable. However,
without caution it could be much worse. Be cunning and careful.
TIME: *A difficult time, one thing comes to an end and nothing else is ready to
take its place. Be patient and watch developments.*

Path 5.6/2 ☺

**The carriage loses its curtain.
Do not go back for it
In seven days it will be replaced.**

Something that is a lot of effort now will be much easier later on.
Don't worry about superficial problems ('curtains'), they can be
dealt with later. If you've lost something, it will be returned.
TIME: *Your position is improving and there's nothing that you need to do except
be careful to avoid set-backs. Be cunning and cautious.*

Path 5.6/3 ☺☺

> The illustrious ancestor
> Disciplines the devil's country.
> In three years he conquers it.
> Inferior people should not be employed.

The only really active Path in this Situation. You can overcome difficult problems. Act bravely.

TIME: *Lucky, but unsettled. Your star is rising, put plans and changes into effect.*

Path 5.6/4 ☹

> The finest clothes turn to rags.
> One slip and they are ruined.
> Be constantly vigilant.

Things that you rely on let you down, you can survive only if you are very cunning. Smart clothes will not help you when things get rough. If you try anything, it will fail and you'll lose what you have.

TIME: *You could lose a great deal during this time. Only by being extremely careful can this be avoided.*

Path 5.6/5 ☺

> The eastern neighbour who slaughters an ox
> Does not attain as much real happiness
> As the neighbour in the west
> With his small offering.

Small matters go well, important ones should be put on hold.

TIME: *Pretentious displays get you nowhere but steady work will bring fair rewards.*

Path 5.6/6 ☺

> He gets his head in the water. Danger.

This is the very end of the crossing and it's easy to get careless and slip up.

TIME: *Your affairs will improve soon, don't get jumpy and make mistakes.*

Situation 5.7 Rain on the Mountains

The pass is blocked.
Retreat and seek counsel.
Make no changes yet.
Another way can be found.

Firm Purpose (mountains) in the House of Adversity (rain). This relationship just doesn't work. Copy Firm Purpose, stay still and keep out of trouble.

Rain makes the mountains impassable. It is pointless to fight nature. You can wait for better weather or take another route. There is no shame in delay that is beyond your control. If you press ahead the difficulties will increase until you're forced to halt. It is time to stop and rethink, and take professional advice if appropriate. There is always another way round.

Path 5.7/1 ☹

The pass is blocked with mud.
Retreat is favourable.

No point in moving ahead just now, withdraw and keep out of trouble.
TIME: *You are in a very weak position and can't do much at all. Stay within your limits and all will be well. Study and other quiet pursuits go well.*

Path 5.7/2 ☺

In a noble cause.
Struggling through the rain.
Many obstacles.
No fault of yours.
Good fortune in the end.

This Path is the only one in this Situation that can be followed rigorously. It's not a Path that one would necessarily choose, but it's one of the rare instances where you can face danger head on and win. Unorthodox methods are quite acceptable on this Path, provided your cause is just.
TIME: *Now you can overcome any seemingly insurmountable problems in your life.*

Path 5.7/3 ☹

Great rocks obstruct the pass.
Return.

Even if you are in the middle of something, it's better to withdraw, for the time being at least.
TIME: *You are in a time of transition, but must hold back for the time being. This is stressful.*

Path 5.7/4 ☹

The mountains cannot be crossed.
Retreat and join with others.

Not a good Path to follow. Postpone or abandon plans.
TIME: *A time of stagnation that must be endured while preparations are made for future progress.*

Path 5.7/5 ☹

In great difficulty help arrives.

This is not a Path of choice, but you can follow it if you have to. Look for help.
TIME: *Quite positive, but there are some hidden snags that need sorting out. It's important that you are contactable or you may miss important warnings. If you have things planned make enquiries and double check things. Friends will be helpful.*

Path 5.7/6 ☹

Advance is blocked.
Retreat is favourable.

Seek wise counsel. You are in an ambiguous position; you would like to look after your own interests, yet you have responsibilities that are hard to overlook. Think very carefully about how to balance these factors, but in the end you must do what you *feel* is right.
TIME: *Many difficulties and some good opportunities. A time to be brave and to realize that you cannot please everyone. Above all you must be true to yourself.*

Situation 5.8 Constraint

**Held within the courtyard.
Become strong in safety.
Good fortune.
Do not tarry long.
The fruit in the garden will turn sour.**

*Escape in the House of Adversity. This is a relationship that serves
a purpose, once the purpose is completed the relationship should end.*

Responsibilities are a mixed blessing. On the one hand their being
constrained keeps you out of trouble and develops character, and on
the other it stunts growth. When you receive this Situation,
constraint is good for you and you should bear it with patience
for the time being. However, don't let it become a permanent thing,
for this will stunt your emotional growth and lead to bitterness.

Path 5.8/1 ☹

**Safe within the courtyard.
No blame in remaining.**

There is no need to leave the courtyard at present, if you try you will
waste your strength. It will not be difficult to back out of arrangements.
TIME: *Your position is very weak. Don't be tempted to weaken yourself further.
Live very quietly and better times will come.*

Path 5.8/2 ☺

**Life in the courtyard is stale.
It is time to look outside.**

Too strict limits have been placed on you for too long. This isn't an
easy Path to follow because you have a lot of inertia. You may not
be able to find the right things to do straight away. However, a
start must be made before you become totally immobile. You need
to act boldly, drop your plans, and come up with something more
exciting.

TIME: *Forget your responsibilities and break free from constraint. Now is the time to try out new ideas. Let your hair down, enjoy yourself.*

Path 5.8/3 ☹

The courtyard is dull.
But there is danger outside.
Someone with no patience will suffer.

You may be feeling restless and so be tempted to try to hurry things up. This is not a good idea, let things develop at their own pace and you may find some success.

TIME: *You will be restless, but it's vital that you keep steady otherwise you'll lose your direction.*

Path 5.8/4 ☺

Responsibilities to fulfil.
Do not leave in a hurry.

You are fine as you are for now, do not act. An offer may look good, but it is better avoided.

TIME: *Carry on as you are and your life will be stable. You can make steady progress for quite some time yet. Changes will be needed in the long run though.*

Path 5.8/5 ☺

Working in the courtyard
There will be much to show.

Stick to your work. Do not act. An offer may look good, but it is better avoided.

TIME: *This is a time to work hard to improve your future. Stick to what you do best and keep a steady rhythm. Don't let things slip, or burn yourself out. A good sustained effort now will lead to much better times.*

Path 5.8/6 ☺

Exceptional efforts.
Matters must be put right.
Harsh, but only for a little while.

Here, for a short period, you must put yourself into some form of harsh discipline. It could be giving up a bad habit, doing some horrid task you've been avoiding or something else. A show of strength and self-discipline now will benefit you for years to come. Once you've finished doing what needs to be done, return to normal. Some people find being in 'emergency' mode exciting, but this isn't good in the long term as it damages your health and relationships.

TIME: *You are in need of strong constraint and you won't like it. Stick with it and you can free yourself up later.*

6. The House of Intensity

The heat of midday.
Let your true nature shine
Then your passion will be
your guide.
One who sits in the hot sun
all day will surely suffer.

The House of Intensity is about letting your true nature shine. Then you can act with great passion and commitment in whatever you do. To do this you must follow your feelings, for there can be no real passion without inner affinity.

There are many things that must be done while you are in the mood otherwise they won't be done at all. In this House time must be used to the full, and that should not be allowed to delay you in your quest for fulfilment. Any losses incurred will be more than justified by the success of your actions.

Intensity by its nature doesn't last long and it is important to know when to stop, hence the warning not to sit in the sun all day.

Situation 6.1 Harmony

Brilliant sunshine.
A big wagon to load.
Even the hidden corners are illuminated.

Challenge (metal) in the House of Intensity (fire). A lovely combination. Intensity softens the inflexible Challenge. Brilliance and strength can do anything.

This Situation is three times favourable. It is a happy time (sunshine) that should be enjoyed while it lasts. You can succeed in an undertaking (wagon). Also it's a time when spiritual practice ('light in hidden corners') can be developed and can be of benefit for a lifetime and maybe beyond!

The power of this Situation is rather limited so its benefits often don't last long. Usually it refers to periods of excellence that should be used to the full. On the other hand if you are asking about something serious and long-term, then you have very good prospects for some time to come.

Path 6.1/1 ☺☺

**Pure merit
Cannot be harmed.
Even dangerous things are safe.**

Act naturally and nothing will harm you, if only life was always like this. Pleasure brings good luck. A project will be successful, though there will be difficulties at first.

TIME: *Generally pleasant and prosperous, work to ensure continuing prosperity. Sometimes it refers to a time of danger, when matters work out better than expected.*

Path 6.1/2 ☺☺

**Great rewards.
Load a big wagon.**

You can do something on a grand scale in safety and be successful.
TIME: *A time of enjoyment and profit; use it well.*

Path 6.1/3 ☺☺

Sincere in a good cause
Even a fool has merit.
You will be tested
Then rewarded beyond expectation.

You must do what you're best at, diligently, and let fate take its course. Fate is very favourable for you. The bit about the 'fool' means that when you do good things with a good attitude your personal weakness is forgiven.

TIME: *You may be in a difficult situation and tempted to give up your principles to patch things up. This would be a mistake, this is just a test and you will be well rewarded if you stick to your course.*

Path 6.1/4 ☺☺

Keep your distance from others.
Success attracts envy.
Modesty in receiving rewards brings good fortune.

All goes well but there is the danger that success will inspire jealousy. Counter this by maintaining a dignified and modest exterior. This warning is not meant to put you off, just to make you more aware.

TIME: *Pretty good, enjoy it while it lasts. Look for things of lasting value.*

Path 6.1/5 ☺☺

Beyond reproach.
Great merit with dignity.
Let your light shine.

A project will be very successful, so move ahead with confidence.

TIME: *Most matters will go very well, and life is good.*

Path 6.1/6 ☺☺

Heaven sees your merit.
Rewards come naturally.

Continue with your plans. This is a very lucky Path.

TIME: *Harmonious and prosperous: enjoy, enjoy, enjoy.*

Situation 6.2 Damaged Goods

**Progressing in sorrow.
A good horse that is lame.
One's destination is reached.**

> *Development (earth) in the House of Intensity (fire). Intensity is damaged, as fire is smothered by earth. It doesn't put it out altogether, just makes it miserable.*

This can be hard to interpret. 'Damaged goods' means things are intrinsically valuable but have been damaged in some way. Provided you know this in advance and can make allowances all goes well. For example: you see a fine old vase in a junk shop at a reasonable price. Close inspection reveals it is cracked; you offer a lower price and get a bargain.

Another meaning is to do with things being materially good, but your pleasure is diminished by personal problems which take the shine off success. Again if you know this in advance the disturbing effect is minimized.

If you are asking about time (for example; 'What will next year be like?') then you will gain materially in unexpected ways, but suffer some personal sadness.

If you make allowance for some extra difficulties at the outset, there is no reason why you cannot proceed successfully in this Situation.

Path 6.2/1 ☹

**Progress is delayed.
No harm.**

Best to wait for a while before doing anything, there is no need to rush.

TIME: *You can make good progress in small matters, but life is tinged with sadness. Avoid making important commitments. Some unexpected cash may come your way.*

Path 6.2/2 ☹

Progress in sadness.
Consider holding back.

There will be some unwelcome hindrances if you proceed, you can force your way if necessary. Goods will be faulty, but can be fixed.

TIME: *Quiet progress is favoured and you may receive some unexpected gain. All is not as it should be though and real happiness is in short supply. Money will come to you from an unexpected source.* ·

Path 6.2/3 ☺

Be careful about making agreements.
Then there will be no remorse.

There are very good prospects here, but there may be some snags you haven't seen. Be sceptical of people who are overtly compliant. If you are cunning you can proceed successfully. A purchase will turn out to be excellent value.

TIME: *Good progress can be made, but there is darkness in your life. Watch your interests carefully. A very good time for money.*

Path 6.2/4 ☹

Progressing like a mouse
Slow and undignified.

Progressing this way may be better than no progress but it is clearly less than ideal.

TIME: *You can get by and even profit from this time, but things are not as you would wish them. A surprise windfall could brighten things up.*

Path 6.2/5 ☺

Progress with sweat and tears.
Take not gain and loss to heart.

Some progress can be made, but only with great effort. In business you can only profit from someone else's losses. Don't expect easy gains and you won't be disappointed.

TIME: *All right, but there are shadows on your happiness. Work steadily and try to keep your mind off things that upset you. An unexpected windfall will cheer you.*

Path 6.2/6 ☺

**Progressing with the horns.
The door opens then closes.
Awareness of danger brings good fortune.
Strong discipline.
Going too far leads to humiliation**

Bold action will bring success on this Path. This may not be the ideal way of progressing, but it is effective. This is a good Path for getting out of trouble. A purchase will be good value if the price is right.

TIME: *Applying self-discipline at this time will pay dividends in the future. If you're in danger, now is a good time to escape. Extra cash comes your way.*

Situation 6.3 Justice

At the market
Cut the bad meat from the carcass
Then you can eat safely.
The use of force is justified.

Awakening (power) in the House of Intensity (light). A lively
combination, Intensity illuminates the truth and Awakening enforces
it. Neither archetype has much lasting power, so this is probably a
passing phase.

You should not accept someone or something making life difficult
for you. I'm not saying that you should blow up every time you're
thwarted, it's just a matter of making *sure* people see the fairness of
your claim. A bit of passion may be required to persuade them to
listen, that's all. Being prepared to 'cut the bad meat from the
carcass' means that you should not be afraid of getting mucky to get
your rights.

This Situation is generally good for trade, protecting your
interests politely but vigorously is considered normal in business.

Sometimes this Situation refers to rooting out a hidden danger,
traitor, troublemaker or maybe even one's own attitude to problems. The important thing is to pursue the truth relentlessly,
regardless of personal interest.

Path 6.3/1 ☹

Shackle your feet,
Then you will not walk into trouble.

Things just wouldn't work out if you followed this Path. If you insist
on pursuing it you'll suffer.

TIME: *This is a difficult time for you, you can't make things happen the way*
you want. However it is possible to progress by leaving your usual habits and
doing something different for a while.

Path 6.3/2 ☺

The enemy's flesh is so tender.
Your nose will be lost
If you bite too hard.

Things will be easier than expect if you act quickly. It may be that something has been annoying you, in which case you should settle it firmly. However, avoid being too hard on people as this will lead to lasting bad feeling. When bringing something to an end be firm but as kind as possible. Business is good, a quick, sure move brings reward. Something you thought very difficult turns out to be easy.
TIME: *Active and fruitful. Work hard and be firm but fair with people. If you are on your path redouble efforts, if not, it's time to make a new start.*

Path 6.3/3 ☺

Cut out the poison
Then you find rewards.

Good results in most matters. This often refers to something that for one reason or another you are loath to do. You should proceed and be prepared to get your hands dirty to get what you want.
TIME: *A vigorous approach will pay off at this time. Assert yourself and make things happen. There may be some bad feeling caused by your straightforwardness, but this can't be helped.*

Path 6.3/4 ☺☺

Cutting through dry gristly meat
One finds bronze arrows.
Act boldly but be mindful of danger.

Bronze arrows were valuable, certainly worth more than old meat. This means that what you intend to do will bring unexpected benefits if you're prepared to get your hands dirty. Now is a good time to settle disputes, firmly but fairly.
TIME: *Be daring, make things happen. Don't let other people's negativity stop you doing what you feel is right.*

Path 6.3/5 ☺☺

**Cutting through dry lean meat
Finding yellow gold
Be aware of danger.
Good fortune.**

Finding gold in a bit of meat is a lucky chance indeed. This cannot be planned, but is a result of being thorough and firm in what you do.

TIME: *If you put in a good effort you can remove hindrances and start new ventures. Get things on the right footing and put people straight about what you want to do. There is no need for excessive diplomacy.*

Path 6.3/6 ☹

**Carrying on blindly
Deaf to reason
You will get caught in the stocks.**

There is not much danger here if you wake up and do what must be done without messing about. Not good for a new project, you have matters to sort out first.

TIME: *There will be all kinds of problems and it will be very easy to get bogged down in dealing with them. It is essential that you keep your priorities clear, or you will do a great deal but achieve very little.*

Situation 6.4 The Melting Pot

The ceremonial cauldron balances
delicately on an elegant tripod.
The sacred food gently simmers over the
eternal flame.
The ingredients must be pure.
The clan is safe as long as this continues.
If the cauldron should spill there will be
disaster.
Delay brings great good fortune.

Good Hunting (wood) in the House of Intensity (fire). These two are a natural pair, but the relationship is unstable. However, with the right handling, this instability can be turned to great advantage, for it is never boring.

This Situation is comparing cooking to the great alchemy that is life itself. Like life, cooking is complex business, just think of the ingredients and how they were produced. Then there is the fire, the cooking utensils and all the experience needed to use them. When all these diverse factors are successfully brought together we have good food. The miracle is that all this happens every day, and as long as it does life can continue. Should for any reason the process fail no one could live long without eating.

In practical terms this Situation is about pulling the strands of your life together to make a successful whole. You must learn to work at different things at the same time, yet always keeping a single goal. This sounds very tricky, but if you get it right the rewards are great indeed. If you fail however the consequences can be dire.

In many cases things will take longer than expected, so postponing plans is often a good idea.

Path 6.4/1 ☹

The pot is covered with filth.
Scrub it and leave it upside-down.
The child of a concubine has better fortune.

This is a pretty bad omen if you're trying to do something. It's best to put yourself out of action before something does it for you. Some form of cleansing, recuperation, is required. Keep out of trouble and you should be fine. The reference to the 'concubine's child' probably means that starting again after a rest will go well, even though it's from a lower position. Carelessness causes accidents.

TIME: *Miserable, but there will be no great harm if you bear your troubles with fortitude and lead a quiet life. There is a danger of ill health and accident.*

Path 6.4/2 ☺

> There's food in my pot.
> Those around are envious.
> They cannot hurt me if I stay true.
> Sadness and good fortune.

Be prepared for delays, there are a lot of possible twists and turns of fate. In end your fortune will be very good, if you can stick the course. 'Food in the pot' means wealth, but there is some disquiet and unhappiness as well. To stay true is to carry on in spite of misgivings.

TIME: *Unstable, but a time of great potential success if you can exploit circumstances effectively. Important opportunities will come your way and they should be seized. It is also a time of great difficulty, but if you act correctly all problems can be overcome very successfully.*

Path 6.4/3 ☹

> The pot's handle is broken.
> Cooking is hampered.
> The pheasant remains uneaten.
> Wait for rain to fall, then all will be well.

Something is badly wrong to prevent a Chinese eating pheasant. 'Rainfall' can be an emotional release or a change of circumstance. It is better to postpone plans as there is a risk of accident on this Path.

TIME: *There are problems that make it difficult to proceed with your plans. These problems will pass, so there's no point battling with them. The danger is that you will become impatient and try to move prematurely, which will lead you into danger.*

Path 6.4/4 ☹☹

The legs of the pot break.
The prince's meal is spilled.
He is badly scalded.
Misfortune.

A moment's folly ruins years of effort. Here the danger of accident peaks, avoid this Path if you possibly can. Disaster here can be very foxy, it may try to trick you with greed or duty. Do not get involved!

TIME: *There is a very high risk of accident or other unpleasant scenes at this time. It is really worthwhile to use the* Guide *to monitor your every move. The danger tends to focus around your responsibilities, so being extremely selfish for a while is a good idea. Danger stalks you where it knows you are most likely to be. Be unpredictable and elusive even if this upsets people, you can make it up later.*

Path 6.4/5 ☺

The pot is adorned with gold.
The ceremonial food is nearly cooked.
Then it must be distributed fairly.

Allow yourself extra time to do things properly, then the cooking process is successful and you can get to enjoy the meal. This often refers to something difficult brought off with delicate handling.

TIME: *This is a fortunate time during which you can bring difficult matters to successful conclusions.*

Path 6.4/6 ☺

Adorned with jade
The ceremonial pot is blessed by heaven.
The sacred food cooks slowly.

Heaven doesn't hurry and nor should you. There are good rewards for those who perform well on this Path.

TIME: *Good. All manner of tricky problems can be solved at this time.*

Situation 6.5 The Young Fox

It is the spring.
Be like a young fox.
Summon up courage.
Cross the frozen river while you may
The summer hunting grounds await.
Daring yet cautious, if the tail gets wet, no
blame.

*Adversity (water) in the House of Intensity (fire). This represents
an unstable, unconventional relationship that's very rejuvenating and
positive.*

You are ready to make a transition, the time is right, rivers don't
stay frozen for ever. Success beckons and new doors open.

That foxes are cunning is taken for granted, but young ones are
bolder, which means that courage is more important than care.
That the crossing is made is all that matters in the end. Getting wet
in this Situation means minor misfortunes that are more than
compensated for by a good outcome. The easiest way to fail is
not to try.

In practice, plans will be successful in most cases although there
will be some losses. The long-term benefit will often exceed your
expectations. Make your preparations carefully and you'll get a
good result.

Path 6.5/1 ☺

A very young fox
Crosses too quickly.
Its tail gets wet.
Humiliating.

It may be that you are a little too hasty even for this youthful
Situation and should consider plans more carefully. However,
caution must not be allowed to turn into procrastination as it is
important that you act.

TIME: *Time to make changes, be youthful and flexible. Be active, but sensible about what you try to achieve.*

Path 6.5/2 ☺

**Applying the brakes
The heavy cart must travel slowly.**

The image changes from 'fox' to 'cart'. A cart is heavy, not manœuvrable, and contains valuables. With such a load one should plan well and proceed with care. However, this is a time of transition, so don't allow caution to degenerate into sloth.

TIME: *Be positive and put new ideas into practice. There is a temptation to move ahead quickly, but don't be hurried. Steady yourself, and check your plans before taking the plunge.*

Path 6.5/3 ☺

**Crossing a great river.
Before the crossing
Prepare carefully.
During the crossing be
Courageous and firm.
After the crossing retire gently.**

This is often about doing something new or something one hasn't done for a while. There will be some teething problems but with the right effort you will attain your desire.

TIME: *A time of transition and there are difficulties to overcome, but don't let the fact that you don't know quite what to do stop you acting boldly.*

Path 6.5/4 ☺☺

**After the crossing
Stick out for what you feel is right.
For three units of time you succeed.**

This is a very good Path provided you have the enthusiasm to exploit it and the stamina to see it through. You can attain something very worthwhile if you push hard now. Even if your affairs are in a mess, you have the strength and ability to turn failure into success.

TIME: *Unsettled and exciting. You can be very bold at this time.*

Path 6.5/5 ☹

**If your cause is just
It is worth discomfort.**

This Path is practical and reasonably safe, but uncomfortable enough to be little fun. It also has little value as an experience. Not worth following without a good reason. Travel is safe.

TIME: *Not an easy time, but work on things that matter and you will do well.*

Path 6.5/6 ☺

**Setting out bravely
As if from drinking wine.
Danger and discomfort.
Be a little cautious.
You will be greater at the end.**

This Path has a youthful 'devil may care' feel. Unlike the last Path here we have excitement and success. Although caution should not be thrown to the wind it mustn't prevent you from living life to the full. This Path can teach you a valuable lesson for your life.

TIME: *Be bold and don't allow old problems to tie you down. Get on with new ideas. The important thing is to learn and a few mistakes cannot be helped.*

Situation 6.6 Flames

**The sun shines brightly.
Look after your cows
Or what will be left when summer has
passed?**

*Intensity in the House of Intensity. All this passion surely can't
last? Could be fun while it does, though.*

Fire comes in many forms, some are life-giving, some destructive.
There are two main qualities of fire: heat and light. Getting the
correct balance of these elements is what decides whether you have a
candle or a floodlight, a stove or a bonfire.

In practice this Situation has two meanings.

The first refers to a period of intensity that soon passes. This is not
necessarily a bad thing, but there are dangers. By becoming over-
excited you may exhaust your resources, forget to attend to
necessary tasks. If the dangers are borne in mind, a short period
of intensity can be enjoyable and useful. Creative people often have
short periods of enlightenment that set the direction for their long-
term endeavours. Put your energy to work solving old problems.
Holidays serve to break the monotony of existence.

The second meaning is to do with maintaining stability in life.
Cows provide food all year round, this means making provision for
the future. The cow is also a placid animal; if one is relaxed about
life, energy is not wasted in useless worrying. Through clear, calm
thinking the benefits of summer can be exploited fully.

Path 6.6/1 ☺

**The sun is about to rise.
Many trails to follow.
Proceed while the going is good.**

In hot weather the very early morning is an important time for
working. You can get several things done before the day gets too
hot if you put your mind to it. It is unwise to make commitments

though, one should wait to find out what the day has to offer first.

TIME: *A busy time; examine your options and do as much as possible. A good time to shop around but a bad time to buy.*

Path 6.6/2 ☺☺

Bright morning sunlight.
The world looks like gold.
Take your pleasure while you may.

Midmorning in the summer is a beautiful time, the sun is bright, but not yet too hot. This symbolizes a time when things are as good as they are going to get.

Getting this answer often means that you have a window of opportunity. If you have business now is the best time to cut a deal. Holidays will be beautiful and most matters are successful. Do not delay if you wish to take advantage of this favourable Path.

TIME: *Very good for a while so enjoy it. Try to store up some happiness and well-being.*

Path 6.6/3 ☹☹

The fire that blazes soon goes out.
First you beat pans and sing
Then you smash them, and howl in
Frustration
Cursing your own stupidity
Crying at the thought of old age and
Poverty.
Only those who know when to stop will have cause
to smile.

If you follow this Path, at first all seems to go well then you suddenly find you have lost everything. A tempting offer will lead to disaster. If you're not very careful you will lose not only your fortune but everything you care about. Once bad luck has struck it will be too late, you will curse and scream to no avail. Avoid this Path.

TIME: *A bad time that is easily made worse by panicking. Try to stay calm and postpone all decisions until this time has past. Follow this advice and this time will do you little harm. Your fortunes are turning sour, so withdraw from all plans. Stock will get a fair price now but soon be worthless, take this advice and you will be very glad you did.*

Path 6.6/4 ☹☹

Great heat.
Hopes rise, then are dashed.
The ashes of dreams are swept away.

You must withdraw at once. Save what you can, but don't delay. A tempting offer is a trap. All your energy and money will be wasted if you do anything now. Sell before the crash.

TIME: *A nasty time. Everything goes wrong and all sorts of pressures are placed upon you. On top of this you are overemotional and foolish. Do as little as possible, as you are likely to make big mistakes. Avoid travel and any other ventures. At the early stages of this time when things are still OK there may be a chance to retire from harm's way. If in business sell quickly as the market is likely to fall.*

Path 6.6/5 ☺

Toiling in the heat.
Sweat and tears,
Groans of exertion,
The effort is not wasted.

A bit of hard work does no harm provided it's on something worthwhile. Good for a serious project, but a holiday may be more like a commando expedition. Don't expect great success.

TIME: *A time of work and pressure; there may be quarrels, but they will pass. A transitional phase.*

Path 6.6/6 ☺

Illuminated by the spirit.
Working for the Great Plan.
March forward with confidence,
Capturing hearts and treasures.
Many prosper from the work of a
Few.

At the end of the Situation it's time to bring matters to completion. There are great rewards for those who act boldly. Be decisive, the good fortune won't last. Generosity will be rewarded.

TIME: *Good now, enjoy it, but make provision against trouble later on.*

Situation 6.7 The Outsider

A stranger on a rocky road
Must rely on wit alone to get by.
Those of independent spirit are blessed
Even though life is not easy for them.

Firm Purpose (Stone) in the House of Intensity (Fire). This is not usually a close relationship, more of an alliance than a unity. Fire and stone don't really combine, but there is affinity and respect.

Being an outsider puts you at a disadvantage in all your dealings. Those around you have knowledge that you don't possess. They also have contacts to exploit while you are alone. To survive you must be self-reliant and learn quickly, otherwise your life will not be very pleasant.

With practice one can adapt to most conditions, find friends quickly and generally learn to feel at home anywhere. This is what is called making a virtue of necessity and is the main meaning of this Situation.

Path 6.7/1 ☹

When trivial problems fill the mind,
Danger goes unnoticed.

What you have in mind is a waste of time. There are more important matters to attend to.

TIME: *You are in a weak position. There is a danger that you will get bogged down in minor problems while matters of consequence are neglected.*

Path 6.7/2 ☺

A traveller finds a good inn.
The luggage is safe.
There is even a young servant available.

An inn isn't home, but it's still very welcome. A 'young servant' could mean any kind of temporary assistance. This isn't a bad Path and most things go well; however, you will still be the outsider, so tread carefully.

TIME: *A time when difficulties will ease. People will be helpful to you if you approach them nicely. A good time to travel.*

Path 6.7/3 ☺

The inn burns down.
The outsider must sleep in the barn.
Danger, do not lose your servant.

There is some difficulty and discomfort on this Path, but no real danger provided you behave sensibly. However, if you get nervy or quarrelsome you can get into serious trouble. The 'servant' can be a person or anything that you rely on.

TIME: *Avoid upsetting people and make sure your support systems are in good order.*

Path 6.7/4 ☺

The outsider gains a shelter.
Guard your possessions with an axe.
My heart is sad.

It's a shame that you should need to stand over the luggage with an axe, clearly this isn't a five-star hotel. This means that things will be harder than you would like them to be.

TIME: *Take precautions against loss, avoid upsetting people.*

Path 6.7/5 ☺

With a single arrow
The outsider kills the flying phesant.
The King is impressed.
Later there will be rewards.

Kings aren't always keen on strangers shooting their pheasants. You have the chance to make a smart move; it may be cheeky, but if you do it with enough style you'll be forgiven. It is important for an outsider to appear bold, yet not arrogant. Move forward boldly. Travel is favoured.

TIME: *Quite fortunate, try to impress important people.*

Path 6.7/6 ☹

The bird's nest is on fire.
The outsider laughs at first
Then cries in alarm.
An ox is lost.

You seem to be winning the race ('the outsider laughs'), but you push a little too hard and all is lost ('then cries in alarm'). This means that though your goals seem within reach, if you actually try to reach them you will fail. There is something to be gained, however, and if you can be satisfied with second best all will be well. There is more than you think to be lost, so be very careful. Keep your head. Avoid overtaxing yourself.

TIME: *Everything goes well, but your position is less secure than you imagine. Provided you are sensible and take things easy there will be no problems. If you give way to restlessness you will injure yourself in some way.*

Situation 6.8 Stress

Stalemate.
You are not defeated.
Modest progress is possible.
Emergencies can be dealt with.

Escape in the House of Intensity. Not a very good combination;
these two don't trust each other, and neither has a decisive advantage
so civilities over the battlements are the best that can be expected.

This is not a Situation that one would become involved in by choice.
Things don't go disastrously wrong, you just can't do what you want
and time is wasted. People and things play up and generally refuse
to follow their normal working pattern. In practical terms it means
journeys that are so delayed it's not worth going, jobs falling
through, etc. The opposition is usually of a petty nature and if
you really need to do something, you should be able do so. Make
sure you stay calm and allow for extra effort and delay. Very minor
matters often go quite smoothly.

Path 6.8/1 ☺

A lost horse will return.
There is no need to search.
When in dangerous company,
Guard against mistakes.

Stay calm even if things go against you. Be careful not to arouse the
opposition of dangerous people. The 'horse returning' means that
there's no need to worry about things that have been lost, as they
will return of their own accord. Nothing great can be achieved.
TIME: *This is one of those times when nothing seems to work out. However,*
when this time passes things will return to normal, so there's no need to worry.

Path 6.8/2 ☺

> If you meet a prince on your path
> Assist him.
> Otherwise do little.

If you are asked for help, even in a dangerous matter, you will be successful, but don't expect reward. Generally avoid this Path; there's no great danger, just difficulty, and not much to gain.

TIME: *Enemies can easily be made, small problems neglected get worse. Keep yourself to yourself and only help out if asked.*

Path 6.8/3 ☹

> The wagon is dragged back.
> The ox will go no further.
> A man's hair and nose are cut off.
> The troubles will pass in the end.

This commentary clearly comes from a very barbaric time, when a man's nose might be cut off yet everything works out in the end! The meaning is more to do with some loss of face, embarrassment, than anyone being maimed. Nothing much can be achieved on this Path.

TIME: *Generally pretty poor, but if you harden your resolve and work steadily in spite of difficulties you find yourself in a better position later on.*

Path 6.8/4 ☺

> Remaining isolated.
> Avoiding opposition.
> If you meet a like-minded soul
> You may spend time together.

Straightforward enough: postpone plans, keep out of people's way and you won't get in trouble. Look for another lonely soul like yourself to befriend. This friend doesn't even have to be human, it could be a hobby, or anything you can think of to pass the time pleasantly. Nothing much can be achieved.

TIME: *Not the best of times, but some quiet progress can be made.*

Path 6.8/5 ☺

> The ceremony is abandoned
> But the feast is eaten.
> There is no harm.

Although there are set-backs a fair result can be obtained. Anything ambitious is likely to fail, but something simple goes quite well.
TIME: *Not easy. Avoid arguments, difficulties and grand projects. Do only what you are sure you can. Don't worry about what doesn't get done.*

Path 6.8/6 ☺

> Remain isolated.
> One feels one's companions are no better than dirty pigs.
> A wagon seems to be full of devils.
> First there is anger and bows are drawn
> Then the folly is realized.
> They are not robbers, but wish to pledge themselves.
> When the rain has fallen the time will be right.

This may sound like some gothic fantasy, but it's simple enough. When people are stressed all sorts of minor annoyances become unbearable. A friend who eats loudly, for example, might be seen as a filthy pig. In this mood, all strangers are going to be treated as robbers. Fortunately there is still enough common sense left to prevent a serious row. 'Rainfall' can mean an emotional outbreak, this will clear the air. Generally not a Path of choice.
TIME: *Keep yourself calm and the difficulties you experience will pass.*

7. The House of Firm Purpose

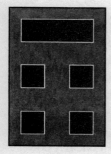

The mountain pierces the roof of heaven
Yet the base is broad.
Even the Dragon cannot shift it.
When the will is set firm,
perfection can be attained.

The combination of height and stability is considered particularly good in terms of character. A person's absolute reliability combined with lofty imagination is quite near the ideal. As far as fate goes Firm Purpose is about sticking to principles, working hard and winning through against all the odds. Not the most fun of the Houses, but good for great long-term achievements.

Situation 7.1 Restraining the Dragon

You have power.
Do not use it.
Eat without sowing
Then the great river can be crossed.

Challenge in the House of Firm Purpose. Firm Purpose is strong enough to restrain even the mighty Challenge, and this turns out to be a good thing. When they are ready they can achieve greatness together.

Here the secret is exploiting the Situation without great expenditure or making commitments. This can be tricky, when one has power it is tempting to use it. Eating without sowing means using other people's resources, which in this circumstance is the correct thing to do. It is a good idea to keep plans quiet until you are ready to put them into action. By carefully saving energy, there comes a point when you are strong enough to cross the great stream.

This Situation has links to martial arts and the idea of strength coming from discipline and restraint.

Path 7.1/1 ☺

Danger is close.
Move carefully.

Difficult, but successful. The danger can be avoided, only invest a minimum of effort.

TIME: *If you are circumspect things should go pretty well, but mistakes could cause losses.*

Path 7.1/2 ☺

Remove the axle
Then the wagon is safe.

By immobilizing the wagon theft is made impossible, also you can't be

persuaded to use it rashly. In practice this often means that modest effort produces modest success, and this is the best you can hope for.
TIME: *Keep a sharp eye on your interests. Limiting your field of action will create success.*

Path 7.1/3 ☺

A horse that races well.
Practise chariot racing daily.
Continue carefully.

This Path has the strength to race, but needs discipline to win. Challenges may be taken, but with a measured approach. Try to see life as a training ground, gradually build skill and confidence as the risk is increased.
TIME: *Be ready to deal with unjustified attacks, and generally be wary of the motives of others. Take a martial attitude, push ahead carefully, and things will go your way.*

Path 7.1/4 ☺

To place a board on a young bull's horns
Saves accidents later on.
Success.

By taking simple precautions now, misfortune can be avoided. Avoid making promises and wait before committing resources. This is a good time to back out of things you are unhappy about without causing too much upset.
TIME: *Generally positive. There are certain precautions that need to be taken. If these are done, this will be a beneficial time.*

Path 7.1/5 ☺

A young boar in a pen.
No harm.
Some success.

A boar in a pen cannot harm itself or anybody else. However, a pen is very restrictive, so this Path is less favourable than the last. Here we must use considerable willpower to succeed. Backing out and taking an alternative should be considered.

TIME: *Apply strong discipline to yourself, then you will do well.*

Path 7.1/6 ☺☺

Time to let go.
Heaven shows the way.
Great success.

You can escape from trying circumstances and leave your troubles behind you. Travel and most other ventures are favoured. While the last two Paths avoid danger by taking precautions, this one does so by not being around.

TIME: *Difficult, but things are improving. Keep calm and continue as you have been for a bit longer, then your luck will change for the better and you can act boldly.*

Situation 7.2 Going Astray

Leaving your true path
The bed is damaged.
Avoid this situation.
No harm if you turn back now.

Development (empty) in the House of Firm Purpose (stone).
Emptiness under heavy stone implies no proper foundation.

This is an unpleasant Situation, all the Paths lead you into danger. The further you go the worse it gets. 'The bed' represents your comfort and well-being, which needs repairing before anything else is done. At this time things will go wrong all around you, all you can do is minimize the effect this has and keep out of harm's way. It might be time to retire, take a holiday or just press on quietly with a solitary project.

The trouble is due to exceptional conditions putting excessive strain on you and those around you and is not really anyone's fault. Under these circumstances it is very easy for you to do and say things that do permanent damage. Retain your self-control and this Situation will pass without any great loss.

Path 7.2/1 ☹

The leg of the bed is cracked.
Go no further.

You are about to stray from your Path. Don't do anything or go anywhere. Put up with difficulty for the moment.
TIME: *Weaknesses are just starting to appear, try to spot them while there is time to take preventative measures.*

Path 7.2/2 ☹

The side of the bed is cracked.
Go no further.

You have strayed from your path and should return to it forthwith.

Don't do anything or go anywhere.
TIME: *Hold on to what you have, as times will be hard. There is no need to worry if you stick resolutely to your path.*

Path 7.2/3. ☺

Deviates without immediate harm.
You can escape without blame.
There is help at hand.

Although this Path leads to trouble in the long run, there may be some short-term benefit. This is because you have a lucky streak; but don't rely on it too heavily.
TIME: *There are many problems, but you are lucky in dealing with them.*

Path 7.2/4 ☹☹

The bed is broken.
The fur covers ruined.
All hope of rest is gone.

You have strayed from your path, but the damage is limited if you go no further. You could get into serious trouble if you do anything or go anywhere.
TIME: *Everything around you is in chaos, people may literally go mad. If it's possible for you to retreat do so, otherwise keep your head and wait for the storm to pass. Avoid getting into arguments, tempers will be frayed and harsh words never forgiven.*

Path 7.2/5 ☺

A fish on a line.
An attractive partner.
Some benefit.
Make no commitments.

This can be a rather tempting Path, there may seem much to gain ('fish' means material gain, and there could be a love interest). It could be worth considering for a short-term project, but beware of commitments. If you stick with this Path your partner will let you down and it will be you that's hooked.

TIME: *Hold on to what you have and you'll be comfortable. Beware of tempting offers. There's no need to worry if you stick resolutely to your true Path.*

Path 7.2/6 ☻

The fruit is poisoned.
The strong drive to safety.
A weak person's house is destroyed.

Avoid temptations. Do not follow this Path. If you have to act make sure you have protection.

TIME: *This is a bad omen for someone weak in their resolve as there will be many difficulties that will need firm handling. If you are strong and determined things will go well in the end.*

Situation 7.3 Climbing the Mountain

**If you can climb the mountain
Don't be satisfied with a hill.
Make sure that you have sufficient supplies.**

*Awakening (moves upward) in the House of Firm Purpose
(mountain). Awakening loves a challenge and what better than a
good hard climb.*

This Situation is about reaching important goals, and not being
put off by difficulty. What is needed is plenty of get up and go,
backed up by a determination to follow through. It may be
tempting to settle for second best, but this is a mistake. Take
care to have everything you need, then nothing can stop you
achieving your goal.

Path 7.3/1 ☺

**Don't whinge and whine at trouble
You will lose your magic tortoise.
Push on beyond the storm.
The effort is worthwhile.**

This is a tough Path, but if you see it through the results are very
satisfying. It takes you through difficulty and makes you feel like
giving up, but if you stay calm and resolute, a way will become
clear. When it's all over you'll have something to remember. The
magic tortoise symbolizes good luck, which may be lost through
whining and complaining.

TIME: *You may have reasons to feel sorry for yourself, but now is the time to put
things right. Stop procrastinating and deal with problems. A brisk, determined
approach will overcome all obstacles.*

Path 7.3/2 ☺

Not tarrying on the foothills.
Look to the summit for rewards.

If you are going to do something, go straight ahead and don't become bogged down in the preliminaries.

TIME: *Some confusion is possible here, but don't be side-tracked from your main objective.*

Path 7.3/3 ☹

Turning away from the summit
Losing one's party.
Delayed for ten units of time.

This Path represents a deviation from what you should be doing, so don't follow it. Concentrate on your most important tasks rather than looking beyond your usual area of endeavour.

TIME: *Poor and difficult, but nothing to worry about if you just get on with things.*

Path 7.3/4 ☺

Making straight for the summit
Eyes as sharp as a hungry tiger.
The way is found, good fortune.

Normally, acting in any way like a hungry tiger would not be advised. Here, however, the end justifies the means.

TIME: *You may have troubles, but there are some good opportunities about. Look out for ways to improve your life.*

Path 7.3/5 ☺

Not much further.
Soon the path ends.
Be content.

Things that you are doing now can be successfully completed, but a new project will not last long.

TIME: *Get the problems dealt with, then you will have a clean sheet. When this time has passed you'll know what to do.*

Path 7.3/6 ☺

The summit is near.
Soon you will have to climb back down.
The achievement will remain.

In practice, this means that you have little time to complete matters. You may not actually be able to finish things as well as you would like to. Nevertheless your achievement will stand you in good stead. A project may not be able to be completed, but it is still worthwhile.
TIME: *Do as much as you can while the going is good. If you work hard now you will have some solid attainments and be able to relax for a while.*

Situation 7.4 Reform

Something has been neglected.
Now it is time to begin putting this right.
Three days to get going
Three to consolidate
Then there will be no slipping back.
You will be stronger than before.

Good Hunting (wind) in the House of Firm Purpose (stillness). Firm Purpose can get stale and Good Hunting is a breath of fresh air.

You can't do everything at once, so something always gets neglected. This is a fact of life and nothing to blame yourself or anybody else for. The thing to do is to get back down to work, and after some initial reluctance you will be pleased how quickly things improve. Once you have completed your reforms you must be sure that they become habitual, allow them some time to consolidate. After that you have nothing to worry about. If you are asking about doing something new, it usually means that there are matters to be cleared up first.

Path 7.4/1 ☺

A son reforms his father's house.
A fresh start brings good fortune.

Some fundamental changes may be needed here, like a son taking over from a father. It is habitual ways of doing things that has led to decay. Do not do anything new until you have sorted out your old problems. Avoiding engagements will turn out to be wise.

TIME: *This is a good time to sort yourself out, give your lifestyle a spring clean.*

Path 7.4/2 ☺

Reforming like a mother
Some sensitivity is needed.

Traditionally mothers don't do things by hard and fast rules. What is needed is a number of small measures gradually brought in and monitored for effectiveness.

TIME: *There are a lot of troubles and loose ends in your life, they must be dealt with patiently. If you're too hasty things will get worse instead of better.*

Path 7.4/3 ☺

Reforming like an angry father
Strong measures bring slight remorse.

Traditionally fathers deal with matters summarily. That force is needed is always regrettable, but in this case it will prove to be the correct measure. Attend to old problems before moving on.

TIME: *Difficult, restless. One might wish to move on, but certain matters must be dealt with first.*

Path 7.4/4 ☹

You are too lazy!
Act like a father, not a spoilt child.

When things are in a mess you must sort them out. If you don't start on clearing them up right away you'll be in a lot of trouble. Don't do anything new. Often this refers to something prematurely abandoned when just a bit more effort would get a good result.

TIME: *Your affairs could sink into apathy and decay, you need to be firm. Work through all loose ends systematically.*

Path 7.4/5 ☺

Reforming like a powerful father.
This is praiseworthy.

A powerful father need not use great force. A few well-thought-out measures, put into practice with firm intent, are all that is required. Clear up old problems and don't undertake anything new until you have.

TIME: *A good time to deal with all the things that have been annoying you for a long time.*

Path 7.4/6 ☺

**Reforming the spirit.
Serve not princes and kings.
Dedicate yourself to higher causes.**

The path to excellence is uncompromising. When dealing with most matters, the wishes of those around you must be considered. Here we have a spiritual need and you must do what you think is right, regardless. Don't do anything new until you have sorted out your immediate problems. Avoiding engagements will turn out to be wise.

TIME: *Do what you think is right and do not be swayed by other people, however important they may be.*

Situation 7.5 Learning

A wise one doesn't seek out fools.
You must prove yourself worthy.
Gold doesn't jump out of the ground.
Even in the right place you must dig.

Adversity (water, profundity) in the House of Firm Purpose (determination).
These two love to figure things out; as long as Firm Purpose is in
charge, all goes well. Adversity is very clever, but somewhat erratic.

Learning doesn't stop when you leave school. Life constantly throws
up new challenges, and you must learn or die. Learning has two stages,
first finding a source of information then making use of it. To persuade
people to teach you useful things, you must prove attentive and able to
make use of the teaching. Decide what you need to know and
concentrate your efforts. You should work hard, but allow yourself
time to enjoy yourself. Whatever you do teaches you something.

Path 7.5/1 ☺

Remove the shackles.
Enjoy yourself.
Then work twice as hard.

Take time off while you can, there will be plenty of work to do later.
TIME: *Not a time when much can be achieved, besides you need time off. Take*
time to live easy, go on holiday maybe.

Path 7.5/2 ☺

Keep the blinkers on.
Attend to your responsibilities.
Suffer fools in kindness.
Maybe you will find a partner.

Get your priorities right and attend to important matters. Trustworthy people can be found and you can safely leave things in their
hands. Use charm to get your way.
TIME: *Freshen up your life, learn something new. Keep your skills up to date.*

Path 7.5/3 ☹

Glittering temptation
Leads to misfortune.
Keep your blinkers on,
Your mind on your purpose.

Excessive pleasure or unsuitable relationships threaten your purpose.
The problem is only temporary, just avoid temptation for a while.
TIME: *Nothing seems to be happening, you become restless and impatient.*
Then all kind of temptations arrive. Don't allow this to spoil things for you.

Path 7.5/4 ☹

Temptation like clinging vines.
The restless become entangled.
Wear your shackles, until it passes.

Sometimes you can't rely on yourself to behave well, the only thing
to do is forcibly keep yourself away from trouble. You'll curse now,
but be glad later.
TIME: *Stay quiet and keep out of trouble. Your thinking is flawed and if you do*
anything much now you'll just exhaust yourself to no purpose. Other people will
be difficult. A quarrel is likely to get out of hand, so apologize now, even if you
don't believe you're in the wrong. You may enter into some unhappy relationship
or project if you are not careful.

Path 7.5/5 ☺☺

The right path at last.
Commit yourself with confidence.
Greatness awaits those with blinkers.

The only danger here is that you will not follow this Path with
sufficient gusto. If you commit yourself now, you'll soon see the
benefits, and the long term is even better. 'Wearing blinkers' means
concentrating all your efforts on a limited field of activity.
TIME: *A very good time for doing something important to you, make the most*
of it.

Path 7.5/6 ☹

Too late to correct mistakes.
Nothing to be done.
Rest, then start again.

Don't be too hard on yourself or others. You are in an ambivalent position. Take no harsh measures. Matters will become clear later.
TIME: *A time when not much can be achieved, take life easy.*

Situation 7.6 Simplicity

**Variation is good
But the theme must remain simple.
Then there is beauty and purpose.**

Intensity (beauty) in the House of Firm Purpose. Intensity brings welcome brightness and variety to the House and if this can be done without compromising simplicity, this will be a good thing.

No creature can live without variety, it is a basic need. Very few of us would wish to live a life where we did exactly the same things every day. This doesn't mean that it would be good to abandon all stability in the quest of endless change – there must be balance. The same meal served with different seasoning maintains excitement without losing simplicity and this gives the meaning of this Situation.

The idea here is to make minor changes that enhance and express the basic structure. In this way something essentially very simple is adapted to suit many different purposes.

Path 7.6/1 ☺☺

**Good fortune.
Leave the carriage road
You can reach your destination on foot.**

Things are becoming stale, a change is needed. There is something better just beyond the horizon. The 'carriage road' symbolizes safety: here safety must be left behind. Time for a new departure. If you're bold now, great things can be attained.

TIME: *It is time to make radical changes. The need to change is often because things are bad at present. If things seem OK now they will deteriorate unless something new is tried.*

Path 7.6/2 ☹

He varies his beard.
Better to keep it simple.
Misfortune.

It is better to stick to simplicity than make ill-favoured changes. Don't waste your time on trivialities. Any project will be a big disappointment. A problem will be bad for a while, then pass.
TIME: *A bad time generally. If you concentrate on your work and don't indulge yourself, things will go well in the end.*

Path 7.6/3 ☹

Too much wine.
Simplicity is lost.
Continue calmly and all will be well.

After drinking, people become excessively happy or sad. Beware of being carried away with fool's emotions. Any project will be a disappointment.
TIME: *A time of temptation and indulgence. If you concentrate on your work and don't indulge yourself, things will go well.*

Path 7.6/4 ☺

A winged, white horse.
Simple adornments.
The marriage is happy.

The balance of simplicity and variety is about right here, and your fortune will be good.
TIME: *Good, look for new opportunities.*

Path 7.6/5 ☹

A wedding in a garden among the hills.
The couple's clothes are poor.
Their hearts are true.

Here, honesty is more important than magnificence. The wedding takes place in a natural place, presumably the couple can't afford a hall. Material resources are limited, but sufficient; though life will not be easy, love will find a way. Accept less than you might have hoped for, it's all you'll get.

TIME: *Carry on simply and with dignity. Enjoy what pleasures you can afford. Don't worry about material matters, you'll get by somehow.*

Path 7.6/6 ☺

Variety enhances simplicity.
Lasting benefit.
Good fortune.

Act with confidence. Here we have the perfect balance of form and adornment.

TIME: *Good. You are on the right track and you have most of the basic elements of success, a few additions will perfect your plans.*

Situation 7.7 Quiet Persistence

Hold still!
Strength through repetition.
Keep the backbone straight.
Stick to your established patterns.
Take no notice of distracting sights and sounds.

Firm Purpose (stone) in the House of Firm Purpose (stone). This is a very solid and reliable relationship on which much can be built.

This Situation teaches how to build character and achievement over a long period of time. Quiet Persistence is not an exciting way to attain one's goals, but it is undoubtedly the most effective. In fact the success rate for those who practise this type of dogged determination is nearly one hundred per cent, essentially only death can stop them.

You can do this by fixing your mind on something you would really like to do and doing it. The trick is never to give up, if things get too difficult simply put the project on ice and get back to it later. Those words have a fatal ring, we have all heard people say, 'I'll finish that when I get the chance' and known perfectly well they never will. However, those who practise Quiet Persistence *do* get back to their projects and finish them successfully. Such people are rare and almost always highly successful, but they have only learnt a trick that anybody can learn. Among my own friends I have seen all kinds of unlikely people do well just because they stuck to something doggedly. Conversely I know plenty of people with lots of talent who get nowhere because they lack Persistence.

In practice the Paths in this Situation (except the sixth) are not particularly favourable. You often receive this reading when you are restless and wish to do something that will distract you from whatever it is the I Ching thinks you should be Quietly Persisting with.

To master Quiet Persistence is to master fate itself, so every time you get this oracle you should give it careful consideration.

Path 7.7/1 ☹

Restless toes.
Restrain them from leaving the path.

Any temptation to leave the slow, sure way should be resisted. Go no further. It is easy to avoid involvement if you back out early.

TIME: *You are in a weak position and can only work patiently at building your strength.*

Path 7.7/2 ☺

Restless feet.
Keep your legs still.
If is a pity that this is needed.

Carry on as you have been. A new involvement may be tempting, but is just a distraction. Here the instincts (feet) begin to move and the mind (which controls the legs) must forcibly put a brake on. In most cases it is good to follow the instincts, that is why it is a pity to shackle them. If people you are involved with insist on taking some foolish course and you cannot stop them, then that too is a shame. Still, better to be labelled a spoilsport than to make a big mistake.

TIME: *Not easy, you have a long, slow Path ahead and would like to take some short cuts. However it is necessary to keep to the slow, sure way.*

Path 7.7/3 ☹

If your hips are too rigid
You will break before you bend.
Free your heart from false pride.

Ease up, you're getting too set in your ways. Firmness avoids confrontation, but rigidity causes it. Go no further.

TIME: *Difficult. The essence of the problem is probably that you have not yet found your true path in life, and until you do you will suffer. You can prevent much of this harm by being more gentle and flexible. You must be understanding toward others even when they hurt you. Back down and avoid quarrels even if you are in the right. Take what is offered even if it is less than you deserve. Quiet work without expectations will be rewarded in the end.*

Path 7.7/4 ☺☺

Move ahead with confidence.
Persistence leads to greatness.
Keep your body steady.
The danger passes slowly.

You are moving in the right direction and should continue for as long as it takes. This may not be an easy Path, but over a long period of time it can bring about a great change for the better.

TIME: *You have many problems and are dealing with them correctly. In the long run you will be successful. Be patient and steady.*

Path 7.7/5 ☺

Keeping your mouth still
Your thoughts ordered
The danger passes soon.

Stick to your path. The danger is nearly past, you must keep still just a little longer. You may think that something must be said or done, but if you speak out you will open a can of worms. If you keep quiet, all will be well.

TIME: *Probably rather dull, but don't allow restlessness to cause you to make mistakes. Quietly doing what needs to be done brings good fortune. Careless talk could cost you dear.*

Path 7.7/6 ☺☺

Firm in purpose.
Step out of the courtyard.
You can reach heaven.

Your work pays off. You can do whatever you wish to. All matters go well.

TIME: *Now is the time to reap the reward of patient efforts. Enjoy and benefit from this time.*

Situation 7.8 Unveiled

The spell is broken.
By moonlight the mountain is a fairy castle
Yet to climb it at night would be disastrous.
Wait for the light of day to unveil cold,
grey stone before attempting it.
Take two small bowls and sacrifice the rest.
Avoid commitments.

Escape (mouth) in the House of Firm Purpose (fist). The fist
holds too tightly, Escape teaches it to let go. When the old way has
been left behind, the new can begin.

When you get this answer you should continue without making
heavy commitments, because it takes time for the true state of things
to become clear to you.

We all like to beautify things in one way or another. It is good to
dress nicely and have attractive ornaments and soft lighting in our
homes. Once in a while though we should look at ourselves naked in
a plain light and take stock. Ornaments can be placed to better
advantage when the structure they adorn is properly understood.

This Situation applies this principle to all matters and through its
action gently makes truth clear to you, spots and all. However,
though the mountain is less glamorous by day, it is much easier to
climb. This is a good Situation for seeing matters realistically and
making down-to-earth judgements.

Another association is with letting go of one thing so that another
can be grasped. This is the only way that profound change can be
accomplished. You cannot keep hold of everything you ever owned,
something must be left behind. This is the true meaning of sacrifice,
leaving the lesser to gain the greater. Bowls are carried by monks to
collect gifts of food and represent taking only essentials.

Path 7.8/1 ☺

Moving on soon is good.
Finish essential tasks and go.
Do not delay too long.
A modest offering is sufficient.

This Path may not offer great success, but it does give a chance to escape old problems. The exact time to act varies, it could be now or soon; you decide for yourself. A new project goes well, business is moderately successful.

TIME: *A difficult transition. Your ideas will be shaken up during this period and there will be much rebuilding to do. It can be a stimulating Path and good for making changes and travelling.*

Path 7.8/2 ☺

The veil lifts slowly.
Don't act like a marching army.
Calmly see changes through.

Take your time and see how things develop, in time what must be done will become obvious.

TIME: *Let life take its course and see what develops. Stick to plain, simple things and all will go well. Remember even fine castles must have good foundations. Studies and spiritual practices progress well.*

Path 7.8/3 ☹

Beneath the fine cloth the offering is poor.
Three travel, but one is lost.
A lone traveller finds a friend.

Here a handsome mask covers a plain face, which will come as a bit of a shock. In practice this means you are not nearly as secure as you thought. When all around you things are failing the best thing to do is to go your own way and leave troubles to others. You will find new friends and helpers in due course.

TIME: *Sadness and loss. That which you thought reliable lets you down. Here we have the essence of the Situation; a large party, or someone with many possessions, will suffer loss. Someone who has nothing will gain. If you wish for success on this Path leave all your baggage, emotional as well as material, behind. Consider travel or starting something new.*

Path 7.8/4 ☺

The veil slowly lifts.
Reducing the fever brings recovery.
Reducing resentment brings happiness.

This Path is about growing strong by letting go of things that weaken you. Allow things to happen, but make no commitments until you are sure of what you are getting involved in.

TIME: *A time when the underlying truths become apparent. Let go of all that is holding you back. Studies and spiritual practices go well.*

Path 7.8/5 ☺

Releasing the lesser to take hold of the greater.
Ten oracular tortoises agree.
Action is favourable.

Tortoise shells were used for divination in the old days. The principle here seems to be that if you act correctly, you always get a good result, all oracles will agree. Follow this Path's advice and good fortune will be with you.

TIME: *A good time to start something new. Think about what the core activities of your life are, strengthen them, and decrease all else. Then you will have great good fortune.*

Path 7.8/6 ☺

If you can gain by helping others
Others will serve you.
Leave the old ways behind.

Good, but not great for most matters. Following this Path may benefit others more than it benefits you, but that is not necessarily a bad thing. Now is a good time to make yourself useful, later you will be rewarded.

TIME: *Try to get out in the world and make yourself useful, there is much to gain from unselfish conduct.*

8. The House of Escape

The lake is mysterious.
The firmament reflected on its surface
Gives no clue of its inner nature.
In the misty marsh the outlaws live in safety.
Excellence is found by escaping the ordinary.
Leaving while the going is good leads to great success.

The concept of escape is a little hard to grasp. We are led to believe that it is by acquiescing to the demands of friends, family and society that we prove our worth. Suppressing our fears and desires to serve others is called honourable when in reality it is merely convenient. Much of the time it is good to follow the path of convenience, but there comes a time when you must escape from the fate others have made for you and strike out on your own. To know when you have done enough is wisdom, to follow your heart is courage.

In practical terms this means getting strong by doing what you enjoy and breaking free from what other people tell you to do. For example, if someone with acting in their blood doesn't express themselves by acting, they'll never be happy. Only by overcoming our fears and following our true nature can we escape the numbing effects of life in the mundane world.

Situation 8.1 Escaping Defeat

 The army that has won many victories faces defeat.
To fight on is folly.
Remaining behind brings ruin.
The end is near, but not imminent.
Some territory is lost, but life and treasure is protected.
Leaving one battle to fight another brings great success.

Challenge in the House of Escape. These two are not good together at all, Challenge will try to injure the elusive Escape if it gets a chance.

There are two meanings here. The first is to do with withdrawing from struggles you have been involved in. The second is about taking on fresh challenges.

This is a dangerous and unstable Situation. You have done well against the odds and made gains, but the tide is turning against you. If you withdraw resolutely before the storm breaks you'll keep much of your spoils, and maintain your honour. Leaving it too late will bring disgrace and ruin. Having escaped in good form you are then in a good position to make advances in new areas of endeavour.

In spite of the danger, by staying calm and avoiding conflict matters will end successfully. Just before the end things often go well, lulling the foolish into a false sense of security. You may benefit from this ignorance if you are shrewd in your dealings. If you have a business, sell up, you will get a fair price, but soon the market will fall. You must be very careful who you confide in and you should appear confident until the moment you escape.

Family and friends must be handled diplomatically. There is money to be made, but it is easily lost again. Travel is inadvisable and there's a general risk of accident and loss.

You often receive this answer when trouble is about to come to a head and there's nothing you can do about it. You can, however, get out of the way, then it will be someone else's problem.

Path 8.1/1 ☹

Injured in the toes.
Too weak to fight.
Stay safely at home.

Restrict your activities, no good will come from anything you do now. Suppress any restless desires, small follies may lead to serious consequences. Beware of accidents. 'Injury to the toes' is not too serious, but it stops you from going further.

TIME: *The world is filled with troubles and you are not strong enough to help. You must do as little as possible, then you will come to little harm. Beware of accidents.*

Path 8.1/2 ☺

Injured in the leg.
Cries of alarm.
Fighting at night.
Withdraw in time
Then there is nothing to fear.

You are strong and in control at the moment, but things will turn against you soon. Follow this Path only for a short time.

TIME: *Apparently quite good, but you easily lose everything you have worked for. The signs of trouble are there to see, don't ignore them. You will need cunning and resolution to extricate yourself from danger, but if you do escape the rewards will be great.*

Path 8.1/3 ☹

Injured in the face.
Soaked to the skin.
Withdraw or be disgraced.

The reference to the face suggests stubborn pride that leads you to foolishly face danger you should avoid. The disgrace is that you let your friends down by refusing to save yourself. This need not happen! Withdraw and all will be well.

TIME: *Difficult. It is likely that you will be restless and determined to tackle problems head on, but this will be a disaster. Better to turn your attention to other matters until the storm passes and good times return.*

Path 8.1/4 ☹

No skin on the thighs, but insists on walking.
Deaf and more stupid than a sheep.
Head this warning and you will not suffer.

A person with 'no skin on the thighs' should not walk. A sheep that's in trouble has the sense to be led home, but when someone is stubborn they hear no advice. This colourful language means that though it appears you are obliged to do something, if you do some nasty mishap will befall you. There's no reason why you shouldn't avoid danger if you listen to this advice.

TIME: *Avoid action as far as possible, even though it seems you must act, then you'll be spared harm. When this time is over and if you've managed to stay out of trouble, things will go very well indeed. Home is the safest place. Beware of accidents.*

Path 8.1/5 ☺☺

Agile as a goat,
Escapes with ease.

This is a strong omen, it can show the way to escape from the things that tie you down. It is good to travel or do something new. If you have few commitments when trouble comes, you can move on easily. The people you are involved with are about to suffer misfortune, you are only a minor player so have no responsibility. You are free to leave for better things.

TIME: *During this time, a window of opportunity exists and you should take it. If you fail to, you'll regret it.*

Path 8.1/6 ☺

Waiting to leave.
No cry of warning.
Tears are left behind.

It is difficult for you to escape just yet, but it's good to be prepared.
TIME: *This is a time when to escape soon is vital. However, there are usually things to finish off first. There is a danger you will get panicky and try to escape prematurely. Be patient and determined then you will need no further warning.*

Situation 8.2 Withdrawing

The Ruler withdraws into the temple.
Gather your harvest while you may.
Make it safe from thieves and weather.

*Development (harvest) in the House of Escape (autumn). Both
these archetypes are associated with autumn, which is a time of
gathering the harvest and withdrawing before the winter.*

This Situation is about gathering, storing and preparing. You often
receive this answer when you are planning to expend your energy
and the *Guide* thinks you should be saving it. The reason for saving
energy is so that you can make a big advance later on.

Path 8.2/1 ☺

You are uncertain.
Is it withdrawal? Is it advance?
Your grasp slips, but is regained,
Stronger than ever.
You laugh, with nothing to fear.

Some confusion here over what should be done. Once you have
made up your mind you will be stronger in your purpose than ever.
Ultimately this Path must be interpreted according to your circumstances.

TIME: *A time to prepare and train. Maybe your life has become dull and
unfocused. This is a good time to focus your efforts on what you are really best
at. If you do this your life can be transformed for the better.*

Path 8.2/2 ☺

Allow yourself to withdraw.
A sincere small offering.
Good luck.

Examine any proposal carefully before acting. A modest effort will produce better results than a great one.

TIME: *A good time for thought and study. Look for ways to improve your life in the long term. A 'small offering' means there is no need for great sacrifices, it's a matter of showing a respectful attitude.*

Path 8.2/3 ☹

> Slow to withdraw.
> Tears and sighs.
> It is not your fault, but
> No good will come of it.

Plans made that involve people will end in confusion. There is nothing wrong with your approach, but circumstances or people just make it impossible. Press on independently with your life. A project will fail.

TIME: *Unsettled, nothing goes quite right. If you can control restlessness progress can be made. Studies and spiritual practices go well during this time.*

Path 8.2/4 ☺

> Withdrawal not advance.
> Trying to grasp more does lasting
> Damage,
> A danger is still easy to avoid.

Something tempting leads to very bad consequences, if you avoid it you will be very lucky. Pushing ahead will lead to a misfortune that will dog you for a long time. Forget the matter now and all will be well. Any plans lead you into trouble. Avoid action.

TIME: *A time of transition. If you work steadily and look after your interests, you could do well.*

Path 8.2/5 ☺

Withdrawing with dignity.
Someone does not wish you success.
A call is answered.
Lucky in the end.

Your position is strong and you can act independently, though this may upset some people. Having a detached viewpoint will lead you to the right decision.

TIME: *If you work hard and look after your interests you could do well. It is good to advertise yourself to new people. Beware of people you know who may oppose you. Studies go well, and business will be fair.*

Path 8.2/6 ☹

Failing to withdraw.
Tears and sighs.
Hold on and the danger will pass.

It may end in tears if you act now, it would be better to withdraw.

TIME: *A long and difficult phase draws slowly to an end, but it is not time to relax yet, things can easily go wrong. Emotions may get stirred up, if you keep reasonably calm no great harm will be done.*

Situation 8.3 The Quest

For too long you have held back.
Now the time is right to overcome your fears.
Aim high
Lest you fall short of the target.
Then something will be achieved.

Awakening in the House of Escape. It's a powerful combination, these two love challenge and care little for responsibility. If something annoys them they just walk away and to hell with the consequences.

Something you do will be harder than expected, but the results will make it worthwhile. You should go beyond your normal boundaries in search of experience. A great deal can be achieved now and a good precedent set for the future.

A quest may take many forms. Essentially it is about leaving petty troubles behind and fulfilling your inner wants or needs. This is escapism in the true sense, freeing yourself from the demands of society and becoming your own person. Commonly it is something you really *want* to do, but are not spirited enough to implement. You may use all manner of excuses, like, 'It's too expensive, silly, embarrassing or just too much bother,' but this is just cowardice. A warrior takes what is on offer without guilt or greed.

Often in this Situation some sort of conflict of interest prevents you from following it all the way. Not fully attaining the goal leaves some sadness, but you will be wiser next time. Those who don't try never fail, so there's no need to be hard on yourself if after making a good effort you fall short of the target. Grand and romantic goals are seldom fully attained, but the attempt is always worthwhile.

When you get this prediction, it's good to make sure all your commitments have been attended to, leaving you free to pursue the Quest to its limit.

Sometimes you get this Situation when you are having difficult dealings. In this case it means you should gently but firmly get to the bottom of the matter. Taking punitive action is usually inappropriate.

Path 8.3/1 ☺

> Successful quest.
> Going out in company.
> Changing the rules.
> Deeds not words.

This is a good Path for you to follow. Take it as far as you can.
TIME: *Put old fears and worries behind you and show what you are capable of.*

Path 8.3/2 ☺

> One who holds on to the child
> Never grows up.

There are two main interpretations; the first is do with sacrificing something small to attain something great, the second is about making a great effort to overcome old problems.
TIME: *It would be easy to let things slip, but what is really needed is a good hard push in the right direction. You need to be a little ruthless about doing what you think is right, minor problems can be dealt with later.*

Path 8.3/3 ☺

> Holding on to the adult.
> Leaving the child behind.

You can make yourself a stronger person by bold, well-considered action now.
TIME: *There will be problems that have to be dealt with. Firm action now saves much trouble later on.*

Path 8.3/4 ☺

> The quest is successful.
> Going off in pursuit brings harm.
> Be sincere in your purpose.
> The thoughts must be clear.

When things go well, it is easy to make mistakes. 'Going off in pursuit' means either being distracted from your major purpose or going far beyond what is necessary.

TIME: *A good time, when much can be achieved.*

Path 8.3/5 ☺☺

Following a star,
Sincere quest.

A star is a high goal that can never be fully attained, but sets a standard of excellence. There may be difficulties that put you off this Path at first, but you should not be deterred. There are delightful and meaningful experiences if you push ahead. Make arrangements to cover your commitments as you will want more time than you planned for.

TIME: *Very good, much achievement is possible. Think hard about what you really want to do and do it!*

Path 8.3/6 ☺

Honoured like a king.
Make new connections.
Enjoy the benefit while it lasts.
Moving on brings good fortune.

This Path may have a difficult start and you will need to go beyond your original remit. However, if you push boldly ahead you will be glad you did. Allow yourself extra time to fulfil your goals.

TIME: *Good, so make the most of it, do something really good and enjoy yourself.*

Situation 8.4 The House is Saved

The house is in danger,
It can be saved.
The roof is too heavy for its supports,
It must be strengthened.
Find new ways of dealing with old problems.
Decide what to do,
Do not allow anyone to weaken your
resolve.

*Good Hunting in the House of Escape. This is an unorthodox
relationship with intense chemistry, it can be good or bad.*

Here we have chance to avoid danger and make gains by acting in
accordance with the advice given. If you behave correctly now you
will save yourself a lot of trouble in the long run and profit from the
experience.

Good Hunting is associated with wind and Escape with marshes,
so we have a windy marsh. This sounds like dangerous territory, but
luck is on your side and in spite of difficulties you can succeed.

To benefit from this Situation you must be flexible and quick to
react. You may have to use unorthodox methods, but it will be
worth it. This is an unusual time so it is quite all right to bend the
rules as far as necessary for the time being.

Path 8.4/1 ☺

When an offering is laid on white
Rushes
The Ancestral Spirits give their
Blessing.
An endeavour can be successful.

Take a sincere and careful approach. Difficult things can be undertaken if the proper precaution is taken. Travel and studies go well. A
danger will not actually affect you and you need take no action.
TIME: *Life progresses well with proper care.*

Path 8.4/2 ☺☺

**The roof of a dry old willow,
Sprouts new shoots.
In time there will be fruit.
An old man marries a young woman.
They raise children successfully.**

An unorthodox arrangement works much better than might be expected. An illness is cured. A romance goes well even if the couple appear ill suited. Money can be made. A new start will be rejuvenating. A young woman can have children by an old man, this means that an apparently unsuitable relationship will be productive as well as pleasant. The 'new shoots' are delicate at first, don't expect too much too soon.

TIME: *This is often a time of recovery after bad times. Rest and enjoy your good fortune. If you have a good idea you may start it now.*

Path 8.4/3 ☹☹

**If the roof beam gives way
The house collapses.**

An unexpected change for the worse. Things or people that you have been relying on let you down suddenly. Act immediately, the worst of the damage can be avoided. Grave misfortune threatens. It will be expensive in some way to put things right, but you must find the necessary resources. Do not take on any new projects.

TIME: *You are taking on more than you can cope with. You should make changes in your life before you get into serious trouble. Make provision for unforeseen problems.*

Path 8.4/4 ☺

The roof beam is braced.

Things turn out better than you hoped. A bright idea overcomes a difficult situation. Accepting help is the wise thing to do. You can ease your situation by acting now.

TIME: *Although in theory you are overextended, you have no need to fear, help will come when you need it.*

Path 8.4/5 ☻

A dry old willow flowers.
There will be no fruit.
An old woman marries a young man.
She cannot have children.

You have only a limited amount of strength and should use it carefully. An old woman cannot have children even by a young man; this means a relationship that may be pleasant, but not productive. Great things should not be attempted. A new project runs into difficulties, existing projects are hard going, but no great danger.

TIME: *You will be tired and find it hard to cope. There is a danger that because of this you will be tempted to do something 'exciting' to take your mind off things. If you do, you may exhaust yourself and make matters worse. You must conserve your strength and be patient.*

Path 8.4/6 ☹

While wading through the marsh
The water goes over your head,
This can't be helped.
The crossing is made in the end.

Although unpleasant, there is no great danger here; proceed carefully and don't let problems put you off your course. Go no further than you have to. Don't take on anything new until you have cleared existing troubles. People will go out of their way to upset your plans.

TIME: *There are some misfortunes that cannot be avoided, but if you are careful there's no great danger.*

Situation 8.5 Burdened

The lake is nearly dry.
Lay your burden down.
Do not act unless you have to.
If you must then the will must be firm as
iron.
Words are not heeded.
Look for something new.

Danger (pit) in the House of Escape (lake). A hole under a lake
slowly drains the water.

Things are going into decline, the image is of a dry, inhospitable landscape through which you must carefully pick your way. Even in difficult territory good progress is possible if you travel light and maintain a firm discipline.

This Situation often refers to a time when a phase is ending and you need to escape and start something new. Water represents both physical necessity and the spirit of enthusiasm. It is no use hanging around a dry lake, so you must move. The 'iron will' is what is needed to fix your goal and make the move. In the meantime, you should cut back on unnecessary tasks, and concentrate on ways to escape.

You should act independently if you wish to succeed, for what you say will not be taken seriously and your actions must speak for themselves.

Path 8.5/1 ☹

A dead tree.
The rut is deep.
Three units of time pass.

If possible, avoid this Path. At best it will be unsatisfactory. Students who lock themselves away to study will do well.

TIME: *Things may seem all right at first, but you are fast approaching a dead end, make changes before it's too late.*

Path 8.5/2 ☺

> Mild suffering.
> You have food and drink,
> But no real purpose.
> A good offer from someone dressed in
> A red garment.
> Make sacrifices to a noble cause.

This Path can be followed fairly safely. A student who studies hard
will do well. Travel arrangements will go adequately.

TIME: *Not easy, but you can get by quite well for the moment. Your life is stale
and if you don't make changes, you will be in trouble in the long run. Look out
for a change in direction and take precautions. You may see or be offered an
opportunity. (In old China officials were dressed in red.) This offer will
involve some personal sacrifice, but it is just what you need to reverse your
decline.*

Path 8.5/3 ☹☹

> A burden like stone.
> Do not lean on thorns.
> At home the loved one is absent.

Avoid taking action at this time, a better way will appear later.

TIME: *You need to make some changes, you carry too much of a burden. Make
things easier for yourself or you'll suffer.*

Path 8.5/4 ☺

> Travelling slowly in a carriage.
> Then one's possessions are safe.
> There is no need for haste.

A difficult Path, but it can be followed without loss if you are careful.

TIME: *Tired but coping. You have enough of everything except joy. Look for a
way to better things. Studies go well.*

Path 8.5/5 ☹

Insulted by those above.
The feet and nose are injured.
Something should be sacrificed.
Then things slowly get better.

You are held back and humiliated now, but not for ever. In order to progress, something must be left behind.

TIME: *You are well placed to survive through the hard times. Look after yourself and your family and in the end you will come through. Look out for ways to make life easier.*

Path 8.5/6 ☹

Delayed by creeping vines.
One is uncertain.
Movement is difficult at first.
But then the way is clear.

Bad times are passing. A way out can be found. Do not act for the present.

TIME: *You have survived through hard times. The important thing now is to make sure that you free yourself completely from the troubles that have afflicted you. If you don't, you will have a very slow recovery.*

Situation 8.6 Breaking the Habit

Big changes should be made.
A prize worth fighting for.
When the time is right
You will be rewarded with a new skin.

Passion (fire) in the House of Escape (lake). There will be quarrels until a fresh start can be made.

What is needed here is good shake up, it is a classic House of Escape Situation. There is a chance to change your humdrum existence for something more exciting. The question is whether you have the sense to take it. Making changes isn't easy and involves risk, which is why most of us settle for mind-numbingly dull lives. The I Ching was designed to help the bold of spirit minimize the risks of following a more romantic existence.

The traditional text talks of being given animal skin as a mark of warriorhood; superficially these were symbols of rank. On another level it would mean a warrior taking on something of the spirit of the animal. The wearing of the skin was part of a process of inner development. In early societies spiritual and worldly growth were seen as two sides of the same coin. To really benefit from this Situation you must learn to improve your inner and outer worth at the same time. When thoughts, words and deeds all accord with each other, anything is possible.

You may not be able to make big changes all at once, the Paths represent the stages of preparing for change. You should try to broaden your outlook, travel and practise convincing people of your worth. At the same time, develop your skills by patient endeavour. Then, when you're ready, take the world by storm.

Path 8.6/1 ☺

Awarded a yellow cow skin.
Held firmly in place.

This is the beginning of the change. A cow skin has low status, it symbolizes docility and hard work. You cannot gain wide recognition yet, but you can begin to see how it can be done. Then with steady work build yourself a good future.

TIME: *Not much success possible in worldly affairs. A good time to travel and broaden your outlook. Learn different ways of doing things and practice convincing people. Alternatively you could work quietly on a project. If you have a hobby you would like turn into a profession, now would be a good time to move in that direction.*

Path 8.6/2 ☺

Your time will come.
You will be awarded a new skin.

This is a fairly reliable Path, though it is better not to hurry.

TIME: *An active approach is needed, shake things up, make changes. Travel and new beginnings go well.*

Path 8.6/3 ☹

One encounters opposition.
Much worry, little danger.
A little initiative brings good fortune.

Not an easy Path, but perfectly negotiable if need be. Small efforts will give better rewards than great.

TIME: *A worrying time, but if you keep your nerve all will go well in the end.*

Path 8.6/4 ☺

Make big changes.
Regret nothing.

A reasonable Path to follow. Small changes are little use, you need fundamental reform.

TIME: *Be active and make changes, don't be afraid to rock the boat.*

Path 8.6/5 ☺☺

**Awarded the skin of a tiger.
You may make great changes.**

A tiger skin is powerful, it is only given when you are ready to act powerfully. Whatever you have in mind should be put into practice forcefully. If someone makes you an offer it will be good to take it. Unorthodox methods may be justified. Great profit from bold action.

TIME: *Moving or taking on new commitments is favoured. You can greatly improve your status at this time. If there is something you have always wanted to do, now could be the time to do it.*

Path 8.6/6 ☺

**Awarded the skin of a leopard.
Refinement
Brings changes to completion.**

Good for most things. Sixth Paths often refer to finishing existing business. Leopard skin is associated with perfection and beauty, rather than great power.

TIME: *Take measures to bring changes you make to completion. Secure and consolidate your position.*

Situation 8.7 Open to Influence

**Misty mountains.
The signs are confused.
Do not act on restless impulse.
Look for a break in the cloud.
The way will become clear.
Let things happen naturally.**

*Firm Purpose (stone) in the House of Escape (laughing mouth).
This is a strange but deep relationship. The serious Firm Purpose
works well with the mercurial Escape. Both are young of spirit and
rather wild.*

This Situation is associated with being open to influences of a
profound or spiritual nature. This spiritual influence enters your
soul and helps you to find your true path. This means that it's very
hard to make plans, for fixed ideas make it harder for the spirit to
communicate with you. One of the main functions of the spirit is to
bring things together, there is a sort of invisible web that links like-
minded people. This power is very strong at the moment and you
will find yourself drawn to others of your own type.

Stick to what you feel is right and a chance will come to escape
your limitations. Be patient and wait to be guided. The Paths have
various degrees of mist and confusion associated with them.

Path 8.7/1 ☹

**The mist is dense.
Keep the toes still.**

Sinister influences threaten you, beware of trouble. If the toes are
still, the rest of you is as well. There is no immediate danger, so it's
best to move very little until the fog has lifted. A project can be
successful for a very short time, make provision to cut and run.
TIME: *Unhappy and dangerous. Do as little as possible till times improve.*

Path 8.7/2 ☺

> The mist is clearing.
> Moving the legs leads to misfortune.
> Staying brings good luck.

The mist is starting to clear, it is tempting to try moving. Unfortunately there is still not enough light to see and some misfortune occurs. At this time it's best to seek pleasant or profitable diversions, as you will be lucky. Later you can continue your journey.

TIME: *Comfortable if you remain as you are, your patience now will be rewarded by favourable conditions later. Trying to push ahead too fast will bring misfortune. A good time for study and preparation.*

Path 8.7/3 ☹

> Running in the mist
> Someone trips you.
> Refrain from restlessness.

Here the strain of waiting starts to tell and there is danger of an impulsive move forward. Don't do it.

TIME: *You are likely to be impatient and tempted to get involved in something you will regret. Remain as you are, your restraint will be rewarded.*

Path 8.7/4 ☺☺

> The mist clears.
> The influence is strong.
> Some confusion, but the way is not lost.
> Only one's true friends follow.
> Great good fortune.

Your instincts are true and you will succeed if you trust your luck. There may be some problems getting things off the ground, but the spiritual influence is so strong that once activated it will guide you. Things that belong together will be drawn to each other.

TIME: *A very powerful time. Do what you feel is right and trust to luck. Make a new start, or travel.*

Path 8.7/5 ☺

> Light mist.
> Wait until it clears.
> Then the back of the neck is set firm.
> No regrets.

Here the mist is clearing and you will soon see which way to go, so keep your options open. The 'back of the neck' is associated with a sense of purpose and once it is set there will be no turning back. This is why you are advised to wait a little before setting your course.

TIME: *Problems begin to clear. Set your sights and concentrate your efforts.*

Path 8.7/6 ☹

> In the mist
> Talking without thinking
> Will bring misfortune.
> Hold on to what is right.

There is some confusion; keep your head and wait for developments. Be careful not to speak too soon or you may look a fool. A party is a success.

TIME: *Considerable self-restraint will be needed if you are to stay on course.*

Situation 8.8 Stand Tall

**Stand tall and rejoice
You have nothing to be ashamed of.
Leave your past mistakes behind.
Stick to what you know is right.
The strong of spirit succeed.
The weak of spirit will suffer.**

Escape (mouth) in the House of Escape. Two pairs of lips can do many things together; provided they don't quarrel it will be a good relationship.

Those who follow their true path are often thought of as selfish, and there is some truth in this. Following your own individual destiny will never be fully accepted in cultures that attempt to standardize human behaviour. This Situation is about declaring your uniqueness loudly and clearly and telling others they can like it or leave it.

The image of the double mouth means that verbal skill is what makes this dangerous coming-out possible. Use your guile, charm and every trick you know to get your way. Of course this will only work if you are sincere about what you are doing. If you waste your powers of persuasion on trivial, foolish purposes they will not work when you really need them. Those around you will grow tired of your empty talk and foolish promises. You must have a worthy objective which you stick to even if it becomes uncomfortable or risky. If you do this, most people will come to respect you and accept your apparently selfish behaviour.

When you are doing what you really want to, obstacles seem merely amusing experiences and no effort is too great. For example, someone who has acting in their blood will happily sacrifice everything as long as they can practise their craft. It isn't only glamorous professions that create this type of joyful dedication, people in all walks of life find pleasure in their work. What matters is that you do what suits you, not your family, your boss or anyone else. Following your own path is seldom easy, there is often opposition and always sacrifices, but if you persist, it will be worth it in the end. This Situation is about doing good and enjoyable things. It is particularly good for careers in communications and entertainment.

There is another side to the meaning, a warning to those who indulge in pleasure for pleasure's sake. If you continue like this you will find it progressively harder to obtain satisfaction. Those who spend a large amount of time and energy seeking pleasures often find only despair.

Path 8.8/1 ☺☺

Standing tall brings rejoicing.
The right path to pleasure.
Go this way in peace.

Follow your star and all matters go well. Even if there are problems, you can overcome them easily.

TIME: *Very good, there is a chance to move toward a more fulfilling life. If you're lazy it will just be a pleasant time that passes.*

Path 8.8/2 ☺☺

Standing tall with sincerity.
Joy sweeps away regret.
Be confident.

Your purpose is honourable and you should continue. Any sacrifice you need to make will turn out to be justified.

TIME: *This is an excellent time to get things off the ground. Be positive and committed.*

Path 8.8/3 ☺

Laughter ends in tears.

Sober up now. What you have in mind is just a distraction from what you should be doing.

TIME: *Seeking easy gratification will make you weak. Your activities need more focus if you are to succeed.*

Path 8.8/4 ☹

Laughter is soured.
No great harm.

This Path seems pleasant enough, but something crops up that wipes the smile off your face. There is no real danger, just unpleasantness.

TIME: *You must think carefully about what your values in life really are. Make sure that what you are doing is actually in accordance with them.*

Path 8.8/5 ☹

Don't celebrate until the work is done.
Be careful who you put your trust in.
Be sober not joyous.

Not an easy Path, there are too many things that could go wrong. It is best to keep moving, do what is necessary, then get out. Keep your guard up.

TIME: *You need to be alert to danger during this time. Focus your activities carefully.*

Path 8.8/6 ☹

Inappropriate laughter.
Don't be seduced.

A sixth Path often means that something is reaching completion. In this case one must not laugh too soon as there may be last-minute set-backs, so be careful. Not good for anything new.

TIME: *Seeking easy gratification will make you weak. If you can keep yourself steady for a little longer you may really have something to laugh about.*